THE WINDFAIRIES

AND OTHER TALES

BY

MARY DE MORGAN

AUTHOR OF "ON A PINCUSHION," "THE NECKLACE OF PRINCESS FIORIMONDE.'

WITH ILLUSTRATIONS BY

OLIVE COCKERELL

LONDON

SEELEY AND CO. LIMITED

38 GREAT RUSSELL STREET

1900

TO ANGELA
DENNIS
AND CLARE
THESE LITTLE TALES
ARE DEDICATED
BY THEIR WRITER

CONTENTS

THERE was once a windmill which stood on the downs by the sea, far from any town or village, and in which the miller lived alone with his little daughter. His wife had died when the little girl, whose name was Lucilla, was a baby, and so the miller lived by himself with his child, of whom he was very proud. As her father was busy with his work, and as little Lucilla had no other children to play with, she was alone nearly all day, and had to amuse herself as best she could, and one of her greatest pleasures was to sit and watch the great sails of the windmill

B

figures like them, and they held each other by the hand, and were dancing and springing from the ground as lightly as if they had been made of feather-down.

"Come, sisters, come," cried the one nearest Lucilla. "See, here is a little human child out here alone at twelve o'clock at night. Come and let us play with her."

"Who are you?" asked Lucilla; "my name is Lucilla, and I live in the mill with my father."

"We are windfairies," said the first grey figure.

"Windfairies!" said Lucilla, "what are they?"

"We blow the winds and sweep the earth. When there are many of us together we make a great hurricane, and human beings are frightened. We it is who turn your mill wheel for you, and make all the little waves on the sea. See, if you will come with us we will take you for a ride on one of the sails of your mill. That is, if you will be brave, and not cry."

"I will not cry one bit," said Lucilla, and she sprang up, and held out her arms.

At once she was lifted up, and felt herself going

higher and higher, till she rested on one of the great windmill sails, and, with the little grey elves beside her, was sweeping through the air, clinging to the sail.

"She is quite good," whispered one, as she held Lucilla in her tiny white arms. "I really think we might teach her to dance, for she has not cried at all."

"No, she would surely tell some one if we did," said another. "Little human child, would you like us to teach you how to dance as we dance?"

"Yes, yes," cried Lucilla; and now they were sweeping down near the ground, and the fairies slid off the sail with Lucilla in their arms, and let her slide gently to earth. "Teach me to dance, I beg. I will never tell anybody."

"Ah, but that is what all mortals say," whispered one who had not spoken yet, "no mortal can keep a secret. Never yet was one known who could be silent."

"Try me," cried Lucilla again, "I will never tell. Indeed I will not," and she looked entreatingly from one to another of the elves.

"But if you did," said they, "if you broke

your promise to us when once you had made it, we should punish you severely."

"But I promise faithfully," repeated Lucilla, "I will never tell any one."

"Well then, you may try," they said. "Only remember, if you break your word to us, and tell any mortal who it was that taught you how to dance, you will never dance again, for your feet will become heavy as lead, and not only that, but some great misfortune will overtake whatever you love best in this world. But if you keep faith with us, then the windfairies will never forget you, but will come to your help in your direst hour of need."

"Teach me, teach me," cried Lucilla; "indeed I will never, never tell, and I long to dance as you do."

"Come then," they said, and some came behind her, and some went in front of her, and some took her arms and some her feet, and all at once Lucilla felt as if she were made of feather-down. She swayed up and down as lightly as they, and it seemed to her quite easy. Never had she been so happy, and she would gladly have danced for hours, but suddenly, just as the sun was beginning to show a red light in the sky, she heard her father's horse galloping over the downs, and in an instant the windfairies had vanished.

When the miller came up to her, he was angry with her for being out on the grass instead of warm in bed, but Lucilla dared not tell him what had kept her, or say that she had been playing with windfairies.

Years passed, and Lucilla never saw the windfairies again, though she watched for them every night. She grew up to be a beautiful young woman, and her father was very proud of her. She was as tall and as lithe as a willow wand, and when she ran or danced it seemed as if she were as light as a feather blown in the wind. There were few people to see her, or tell her she was beautiful, for save the fisher folk who lived in little cottages on the beach, scarce anybody came to the downs. But all who saw her admired her beauty, and most of all her wonderful dancing. Sometimes she would go out on the downs, and dance and run there by herself, and her father would look at her and say: " Heaven help the maid ! I don't know whom she has learned it from, but

I have never seen a dancer who can come nigh her." Then sometimes she would go down to the sea-shore, and this she loved to do best of all, and there she would dance with the waves, and move with them as they slid up to her feet and drew back, and to those who watched, it seemed as if she and they were one together.

The time came when her father wished her to be married, and among the young fishermen and the country folk who came to the mill from the farms across the country, she had suitors enough, but always she said when a young man came to woo her, "First let me see how you can dance, for as dancing is the thing I love best in the world, it would be a pity that I and my husband should not be able to dance together," and as none of them could dance as she did, she sent them all away, saying she would wait for a husband till she could find a man who could dance to her liking.

But one day there was a great storm, and a big ship was blown on to the shore close to the mill, and among the sailors was a young fellow with black curly hair and bright eyes and white teeth, and when he saw Lucilla, he said to himself, "I will wed that girl and take her home for my wife." So one day as they sat on the downs together he begged her to marry him, and go back with him to his own land; he said he would give up going to sea, and would live with her in a little cottage and make their bread by fishing. Then Lucilla said, as she had said to all her other suitors, " First let me see how you can dance, for I will never marry any man who cannot dance with me." The sailor swore he could dance as well as any man in the world, for all sailors can dance, he said, and they began to dance together on the downs. The sailor danced well and merrily, but Lucilla danced faster, and seemed as if she were made of feather-down; and then the sailor, seeing that his dancing was as nothing to hers, caught her by the waist, and held her still, crying, " My sweetheart, I cannot dance as you can, but my arms are strong enough to hold you still and keep you from dancing with any man but me."

So Lucilla married the sailor, and went with him to live in his little cottage by the sea, many miles away from the mill, and as her father was growing old and no longer cared to work, he went with her too.

For some time the sailor and Lucilla lived together very happily, and they had two little children, and her husband fished and sold his fish, and often still, Lucilla would go down to the waves and dance with them as she had done in her old home. She tried to teach her little children to dance as she did, but they could not learn because the windfairies had never touched them. But one winter her husband's boat was dashed to pieces, and the sea froze so that all the fish died, and they became so poor that they could barely get enough to eat. Then it chanced that a big ship came to the village where they lived, and the captain wanted men for a long journey, and her husband told Lucilla that he had best go with him, and then he would have enough money to buy another boat, and then next year they must hope for better luck. So Lucilla was left alone in the cottage with her father and her two little children, and she felt very lonely and sad without her husband, and often she thought of the mill and the windfairies, and when the wind blew, she would go down to the water's edge and hold out her arms and pray them to take care of her husband's ship, and bring it safe home again.

" Oh, kind windfairies," she cried, "see, I have kept faith with you, so do you now keep faith with me, and do me no hurt." And often she would dance by the edge of the waves, as she used to do in her old home, and think that the windfairies were dancing with her, and holding up her steps.

Now it chanced that one day, as Lucilla was dancing on the shore, there rode by two horsemen, and they stopped and watched her as she danced, with the waves coming close to her feet. Then they got down from their horses, and asked who she was, and where she had learned such dancing. She told them she was only the wife of a poor fisherman, but she had danced for long years, since she was a little child, when she had lived in a windmill, on the downs far away. They rode away, but next day they came again, and brought others with them, and begged Lucilla that she would go down to the water's edge and dance with the waves as she had done yesterday. So she ran down the beach, and danced in time to the sea as it moved, and the strangers all applauded, and said to each other, " It is wonderful, it is marvellous."

They then told her that they came from a country where the King loved nothing so much as beautiful dancing, and that he would give great sums of money to any one who danced well, and if she would go back with them to his court, and dance before the King, she should have a sack of gold to take home with her, and this would make her a rich woman, and her husband would never have need to work any more.

At first she refused, and said her husband was away, and would not know where she was gone, and she did not like to leave her two little children ; but still the courtiers persuaded her, and said it would not be for long, and her father persuaded her too, since he said it would make them all rich if she brought home a sack of gold. So at last Lucilla agreed that she would go back with them to the King's court and dance there, but she made them promise that before the spring came they would send her back to her own little cottage.   On hearing this, the strangers were much delighted, and bid Lucilla make ready to start at once, and that night she said good-bye

to her little ones, and left them, to go with the
travellers. Her eyes were red with crying at
leaving her home, and before she started, she
went out alone on to the cliffs, and stretched out
her arms, and called to the windfairies to go with
her and help her, for she feared what she was
going to do, and she begged them to be true to
her, as she had been true to them.

They sailed for many days, till at last they
came to a country of which Lucilla had never even
heard, and to a big town, which seemed to her
as if it must hold all the people in the world, so
crowded was it, and above the town on the hill,
they pointed out to her a royal palace, and told
her it was where the King dwelt, and there she
would have to dance ere the week was out.

"And it is most lucky we saw you just now,"
said they, "for the King is just going to be
married, and in a few days the Princess will
arrive, and there will be festivities and rejoicing
for days, and at some of these you will appear
before their Majesties, and be sure you dance
your very best."

Then Lucilla went with them into a great hall
close to the palace, where musicians were playing

on every kind of instrument, and here the courtiers bid her dance on a platform at one end of the hall, in time to the music; and when they had seen it, the musicians one and all lay down their instruments, and rose together, clapping and applauding, and all declared that it was the greatest of luck that the travellers had met with Lucilla, and that it would delight the King more than anything they had prepared for him.

By and by the Princess who was to marry the King arrived, and the wedding was celebrated with much magnificence, and after the wedding there was a feast, and in the evening there was to be singing and dancing, and all sorts of play for the royal couple and the court to see, and then Lucilla was to dance. The courtier who brought her wished her to be dressed in the most gorgeous dress, with gold and jewels, but she pleaded that she might wear a light grey gown like the windfairies, because she remembered how they looked when they danced on the downs.

When the evening came when she was to dance before the King, she threw wide her window and held out her arms, and cried out, " Now help me, dear windfairies, as you have done before ;

keep faith with me, as I have kept faith with you."
But in truth she could scarce keep from crying
with thoughts of her husband at sea, and her little
ones at the cottage at home.

The hall was brilliantly lighted, and in the
middle on the throne sat the King and the young
Queen. The musicians began to play, and
then Lucilla stepped forth on the platform and
began to dance. She felt as light as the sea
foam, and when she swayed and curved to the
sound of the music, it seemed to her as if she
heard only the swish of the waves as they beat
upon the shore, and the murmur of the wind as
it played with the water, and she thought of her
husband out at sea, with the wind blowing his
ship along, and of her little babies living in the
cottage on the beach.

When she stopped, there was such a noise of
applauding and cheering in the hall, as had never
been heard there before, and the King sent for
her, and asked her where she came from, and
who had taught her such wonderful steps, but
she only answered that she was the daughter
of a poor miller, who lived in a windmill, and
she thought she must have learnt to dance from

watching the windmill's sails go round. Every
night the King would have her dance again and
again, as he never tired of watching her, and
every night Lucilla said to herself, " Now another
night is gone, and I am one day nearer to their
taking me back to my own home and my children,
with a bag of gold to give to my husband when
he comes back from sea."

The new Queen was a handsome woman, but
she was very jealous, and it made her angry that
the King should admire the new dancer's dancing
so much, and she thought she would like to be
able to dance like her. So one evening when
no one was watching her, she put on a big cloak
that covered her all over, and asked her way to
where the dancer lived. Lucilla sat alone in the
little house that they had given her to live in, and
the Queen came in behind her, and took off her
cloak, and bade her be silent and not say her
name, for fear some one should be listening and
know that she was there.

" Now," she said, " I have come to you that
you may tell me, though no one else knows it,
who taught you to dance, that I may go and
learn from them also to dance like you ; for in

the home that I come from, I was said to be the most graceful woman in the land and the best dancer, so that there is no dancing that I cannot learn."

Lucilla trembled, but she answered :

"Your Majesty, I lived in a little windmill by the sea when I was a child, far from teachers or dancers, but I watched the windmill sails go round, morn, noon, and night; and perhaps it is that that taught me to dance as I do now. And if your Majesty wishes to learn to do what I do, I will gladly teach you all I know, and doubtless you will soon learn to dance far better than I."

Upon this the Queen was delighted, and flung aside her cloak, and stood opposite to Lucilla, and begged her to begin to teach her at once, that she might learn as soon as possible. All that evening they danced, but when the Queen thought she looked just as Lucilla did, she appeared to be quite awkward and heavy beside her, and was dancing just as other mortals might. When she went away she was very much pleased, and said that she would come twice more to learn from her, and then she was sure that she would be perfect.

c

In her heart Lucilla was very much frightened,
because she knew that the Queen did not dance
as she did, and never could.   However, the next
night she came again, and the next again, and
then there was to be a grand court ball ; and at
this the Queen thought she would first show her
husband how she could dance.   The King
himself was fond of dancing, and danced
well, although not half so well as Lucilla's husband the sailor; and the Queen thought how
delighted he would be when he saw what a
graceful wife he had got.   As the ball began,
all the fine people were saying to each other, it
really seemed silly to dance after they had seen
the wonderful new dancer, but the Queen smiled
and thought to herself, " Now they will see that
I can do quite as well as she."   When her turn
came she tripped lightly forward and danced as
best she could, and thought it was just like
Lucilla, and the courtiers said among each other,
"Our new Queen dances well," but no one thought
of saying that it was like Lucilla's dancing, and
the King said nothing at all on the matter; therefore the Queen felt herself growing hot and
angry, and she turned red and white by turns.

" That lying wench has been tricking me," she said to herself, "and she has not taught me right at all; but I will punish her for her deception, and soon she shall know what it is to deceive a Queen."

So the next day she went to her husband and said, " Husband, I have thought much of the new wonderful dancer whom we all admire so much, and truly I have never seen any one on earth who could dance as she can; but now I think we should do well before she goes back to her own home to know who has taught her her marvellous art, so that we may have our court dancers taught, that they may be there to please us when she is gone, for really there is nothing on earth that cannot be learnt if it is taught in the right way."

The King agreed, and they sent for Lucilla, and the King asked her to tell him where she had learnt her dancing, that they might summon the same teachers to teach their court dancers. But Lucilla answered as before—she did not know—she thought she must have learnt dancing from watching the windmill sails going round. At this the King became angry, and said, " That

is nonsense, no one could learn dancing from looking at windmill sails, neither was it possible that
she, a poor miller's daughter, could have learnt
such dancing by nature;" then he threatened
her, that if she would not tell him the truth he
should be obliged to punish her, and he said she
should have a day to think of it in, but at the
end of the next day, he should expect her to tell
him everything he wanted to know quite plainly.

When she was gone away the King said to the
Queen, "Wife, if this dancer persists in her silence,
and will not tell us how she has learnt, there is
another thing which we must do. We must keep
her here to dance for us as much as we choose,
and not let her return at all to the home from
which she came."

The Queen was silent for a little, but she felt
very jealous at the thought of the dancer remain-
ing at the court, so she nodded her head and
said, "Yes, but I think she ought to tell us more
about it; for myself, I begin to think that it
is witchcraft, and perhaps she has been taught
by the Evil One, and then we shouldn't like her
to remain here and dance to us however beautiful
it be, for who knows what ill luck it might not

bring upon us?" Upon this the King looked grave, and said he did not believe much in ill luck or good luck, but he should be loth to lose the dancer, so they had better settle to keep her if she declined to tell them how the other dancers were to be taught.

Meantime Lucilla went back to her little house, and wept bitterly. " Would that I had never left my babes and my home," she cried, "for I cannot break my word to the windfairies, and if I did they might do some terrible harm to my little ones or to my husband at sea; yet if I refuse to tell them they will most likely put me into prison, and there I shall remain for my life, and my husband and children will never know what has become of me." And she knelt down before the windows and lifted her arms and cried out, "Oh, dear windfairies, I have not broken faith with you, so don't break faith with me, and come to my help and save me in my trouble."

Next evening Lucilla went again before the King, and he said to her, "Well, now will you tell us what we asked you last night, so that we may send for your teachers, and have others taught to dance as you do?"

"My gracious liege," answered Lucilla, "I can tell you nothing that I have not told you before. Since I was a child I have danced as I dance now, and I watched the sails of my father's wind-mill, and I danced in time to the waves, and perhaps that is what taught me to keep time and step so well. I was dancing by the sea-shore when the travellers who brought me here found me, and they promised me a bag of gold to take home to my husband if I would come and dance at your Majesty's court; and now you have seen me dance, and I have done all I can do, so I entreat you to give me the bag of gold, and let me go home again."

The King was silent, but the Queen was still more angry, and in her heart was determined that Lucilla should never return to her home until she had found out about her dancing. So when they were alone she said to her husband, "It is now quite clear, it is by witchcraft that this woman has learned, and we should do very wrong if we let her go till she has confessed all." So again they sent for Lucilla and ordered her to confess, and again she wept and declared that she could tell no more. Then the King said,

"Well, let us give the woman her bag of gold and let her go," but the Queen stopped him, and said, " No indeed, let us first try shutting her up in prison for a bit, and see if that won't open her lips."

At first the King refused, for he said that Lucilla had done no wrong, but the Queen insisted that she was deceiving them, and that her dancing must be witchcraft, and at last the King began to listen to her. Also he was very angry with Lucilla for wanting to go home, and much disappointed to think he should see her dancing no more ; so he consented, and said that either she must tell him how it was she came to be able to dance better than anybody else in this world, and who taught her, or else they should think her dancing witchcraft, and she must go to prison and wait her punishment.

Poor Lucilla wept most bitterly. " Alas!" cried she to herself, " woe is me, for I dare not break aith with the windfairies, and yet if I do not, I shall never see my husband or my babies again, for I fear lest they may put me to death here."

However, she continued to be silent, and the King ordered her to be put into prison until she should speak out and tell them the truth; and the guards came and led her away to prison, and locked her into a dark cell. It was dreary and cold, and the walls were so thick that she could not hear any of the noises from without, and there was only one little window, which was too high up for her to see through. Here she lay and lamented, and almost wished she could die at once, for she believed that they would burn her, or drown her, and bitterly did she grieve that she had left her home and her children.

Every day the King sent down to ask if she had changed her mind, but every day she answered that she had nothing to say. One evening she sat in her dark cell alone, grieving as usual, when the prison door opened, and there entered a woman wrapped in a cloak and with her face hidden by a mask. When she took off the mask Lucilla saw it was the Queen, and she sprang up hoping that she had come to tell her that she was to be released, but the Queen said, " Now I have come to you alone that you may tell me the truth. Who taught you to dance, and where can I learn to do what you do? If you will tell me I will ask the King to forgive you, and you shall have your bag of gold, and go when you like."

Then poor Lucilla began to cry afresh, and said, "My gracious lady, I can tell you one thing that I have not yet told to any one, that is, that I did learn my dancing, but who told me, or how it was, is a secret that I swore I would never tell to any one. And now I implore your Royal Highness to let me go back to my fisherman husband, and my babies. Alack! alack! it was an evil hour for me when I left my home."

Upon this the Queen became furious, but she hid her anger, and first she tried to coax Lucilla to confess all, then she threatened her with the King's wrath, and then, as Lucilla still wept and said that she could not break her promise, she started up in a rage, and said, "Indeed, it is of little use, however much you love your husband and your children, for you will never see them again. The King has settled that you shall be killed this very week, so now you know what you have gained by your wicked obstinacy."

So the Queen returned to the King, and told him that the dancer had confessed that she had learned her dancing, but she would not say from whom, therefore it must be from the Evil One, and therefore there was nothing for it but that she should be killed. So they settled that first they would try to drown Lucilla, and if she were a witch she would not sink, and the King gave orders that she should be taken out to sea next day and thrown overboard, and also that she should have heavy weights tied to her feet, and her arms should be bound to her sides.

Next morning the guards fetched her, and they bound her arms to her sides, and tied heavy weights to her feet, and they took her down and placed her in a boat on the sea-shore, and they rowed her out to sea, and all along the beach stood crowds of people, shouting and jeering, and calling out, "She is a witch! she is a witch! the King has done well to have her killed."

"Alas! alas!" cried Lucilla, "what have I done to deserve this? surely I have done no wrong to be so cruelly treated. Dear windfairies, come to my help, for in truth now is the time of my direst need, and if you desert me I am lost; but

I pray you keep faith with me, as I have kept faith with you." Then, when they had rowed the boat out a little way, the guards seized her, and threw her into the water, and the salt waves splashed over her face and through her hair; but in spite of the heavy weights on her feet she never sank, but felt as light as when she danced with the waves on the sea-shore by her home, and she knew that the windfairies held her up; and the waves rocked her gently, and drew her in towards the land, and laid her on the sand, and all the crowd yelled with rage.

When they found that Lucilla could not be drowned both the King and Queen were very angry, and said that now it was quite clear that she was a witch, and that she must be burnt, so they must take her back to prison, and arrange for her to be burnt in the market-place. So Lucilla was again taken back to her little dark cell, and she kneeled on the ground and looked up to the window, and murmured, " Thank you, dear windfairies, you have kept faith with me, as I have kept faith with you."

Then again the guards came, and took her by

the arms and led her to the market-place, and
here she saw a great pile of wood made, whereon
she was to be laid, and already men were busy
setting fire to it.   But as Lucilla and the guards

came to the spot, there arose a little breeze, and
it blew on to the faces of the crowd who went
to see her burnt.   The men who were trying to
light the pile of wood, said they could not make

it catch for the wind; when at last it did catch
fire, the flames would not rise in the air, but
were blown along the ground. Still they brought
Lucilla up to the pile, and placed her upon it,
and then the flames divided on each side, and
were blown away from her all round, so she sat
in the midst quite unhurt.

At this the people all cried out, "Now we
know that she really is a witch, since she will
not drown and the fire will not burn her," and
they ran to tell the King and the Queen that the
dancing woman did not mind the fire, but sat in
the midst of it unhurt. On hearing this the
King and Queen came down to the market-place
together, and saw Lucilla sitting on the pile of
wood, and the flames blown away from her on all
sides, and causing a great hubbub; so they told
the guards to take her back to prison and keep
her there, till they could arrange for her to be
beheaded. And again Lucilla bent her head,
and said, "Now I know, dear windfairies, that
you will never desert me, and I have nothing to
fear, for while I keep faith with you, you will
keep faith with me."

By now it was getting late in the day, and

the King commanded that Lucilla should not be
executed till next day, and that the scaffold
should be erected in the market-place, on which
the block should be put, so that all the crowd
might see, and both he and the Queen would be
there. But in order to give her one last chance
that every one might see how fair they were,
the King offered that if she would confess, even
when she was upon the scaffold, who had taught
her to dance, she should be allowed to return
whence she came, and take her bag of gold with
her, and therefore the bag of gold was placed on
the scaffold so that all the people might see, and
the bag was so large that Lucilla could scarcely
lift it.

That evening Lucilla felt no fear, and she
would have slept calmly in her cell, but the wind
was beginning to blow in all directions, and all
round she heard it roaring, and the trees were
bending and breaking in the gale. When the
morning came, the King and Queen said to each
other, " This is the morning when they should
execute the dancer, but it will be hard to get her
on to the scaffold with a gale like this blowing."
However, the guards came to Lucilla's cell, and

took her out as before, and led her towards the
market-place, though they had much ado to get
along, for the wind blew so hard that they could
scarce keep upright in it. All along the coast
the little boats were being blown in to shore, and
there were big ships, which had been driven in,
to take refuge from the storm. But Lucilla felt
no fear, only she looked up to the wind, and
in her heart she said, "Now, dear windfairies,
help me for the last time, and keep faith with me,
as I have kept faith with you."

Near the shore came a big ship with shining
white sails, riding over the crested waves, and
although all the other boats seemed troubled
by the wind, and some were dismasted and
others were wrecked, this boat seemed no way
hurt by it, and the people who saw it called out,
"What a gallant ship it was, and how brave the
captain must be, who knew so well how to
manage wind and water." But when they knew
that the time had come for Lucilla to be beheaded, the people did not trouble further about
the boats, and in spite of the gale they flocked
to the market-place, and crowded round the
scaffold on which was the block.

Then the guards and Lucilla mounted the scaffold, and Lucilla began to fear that at last the windfairies had forsaken her, and she wept and held out her arms, and cried out, " Oh, dear windfairies, indeed I have kept my faith with you, surely, surely you will keep yours with me." In spite of the terrible gale, the King and the Queen came down to the market-place, though they could scarce see or hear for the wind, though all the time the sun was shining and the sky was blue. Then the guards bid Lucilla kneel down and place her head upon the block, and the bag of gold was beside her, and they said, " This is your last chance, speak now and confess the truth to the King, and here is your gold, and you shall go." And Lucilla answered as before, " I have spoken the truth, and there is no more that I can tell, since I have sworn never to say from whom I learnt my dancing."

Then the executioner lifted the axe in the air, but before it fell, there came a sudden roar of wind, and the axe was swept from his hand, and the houses in the market-place tottered and fell, and high up on the hill the palace was a mass of ruins. Only Lucilla knelt upon the scaffold unhurt, for the King and the Queen and all the people were blown right and left, amidst the ruins of the houses, and no one thought of anything save how they could save themselves.

Then Lucilla lifted her head and looked out to sea, and saw the big ship coming in, and she heard the sailors cry, " Heyday, these poor folk are in a sad plight, we had better go and help them," and they all trooped up into the market-place, and the wind troubled them no more than it had troubled their ship. But when Lucilla looked at them, the first whom she saw was her husband, and she gave a great cry, and held out her arms, and called out, " Now, dear wind-fairies, do I indeed know that you have kept faith with me, and saved me in my direst hour of need."

Then she told her husband all that had happened, and showed him the bag of gold, and prayed him take her back to her little cottage and her babies by the sea; and she knew that it was the windfairies that had brought her husband to her, for he told her that whatever way they steered the ship it would only take one course, and the wind had blown it without their guidance straight to the town where she was to be killed.

So Lucilla and her husband took the bag of gold, and went back to the little cottage by the sea-shore, and her father and her babies, and the King and the Queen and all the rest of the people were left to build up their town as best they could, and Lucilla never saw nor heard of them any more, but lived happily with her husband for the rest of her life.

NCE upon a time there lived a young girl called Kesta who was the dairy-maid at a large farm. She milked the cows and made the cheese and butter, and sometimes took them into the town to sell for her master.

On the farm worked a man named Adam. He drove in the cows for Kesta to milk and watched her milking them. As she was a comely-looking girl and did her work well, he thought she would make him a good wife; so one day he said, "Kesta, how would you like to marry me? and then we can save our money and some day buy a farm for ourselves, and I should be a farmer and you should be the farmer's wife, and have servants to wait on you."

"That I should like very much," said Kesta, "but I can't say yes, at once. To-morrow I am going to town with my cheeses, when I come back I will give you an answer."

At night Kesta looked into her glass and said, "I wonder why Adam wishes to marry me? but as he does, most likely some better man would like to do so; it would be folly to marry him till I see if I can't do better. I must look about me when I go to town to-morrow, and see who I can meet."

In the morning she dressed herself with great care in her best clothes, and set out for the town with the cheeses in a basket under her arm. When she had got a little way she passed a mill, and the miller all white with flour stood in the yard directing his men. He was an oldish man, and his wife was recently dead, and Kesta thought as she drew near, it would be a better thing to marry him than to marry poor Adam, so she said, "Good-day, would you kindly let me rest a little?"

"Certainly, my girl," said the miller, "you seem to be out of breath?"

"And well I may be," said Kesta, "such a run as I have had. I've come from the farm yonder, and it was as much as I could do to get away, for the farmer's man was very angry because I would not marry him, and of course I am too good for him, a pretty girl like me."

"Are you really a pretty girl?" said the miller; "let me see, perhaps you are. Well, if you are too good for the farmer's man perhaps you would suit me. How would you like to marry me, and live in the mill-house yonder?"

"I think I should like it well," said Kesta, "but I have some business in the town, and must go there first, so I'll stop here and tell you as I come back." So she said good-bye, and went on her way feeling very merry.

"It would be much better to marry the miller than to marry Adam, but who knows if I may not do better than either, so I must not be in any hurry." So she walked on, and near to the town she met a man on a white horse, and saw it was the bailiff of the great Duke at the Palace. "Who knows but that he may want a wife?" she said to herself, " I can but try." So she sat down by the road-side and called out, " Ah me, what a thing it is to be a poor girl who has to run away from all the men she meets ! "

"Why," cried the bailiff, stopping his horse. " Why have you to run? who tries to hurt you?"

" No one tries to hurt me," said Kesta, " but I have to run from men who want to marry me, because I am so pretty. At first it was a man at our farm, and now it is the miller, who would not let me pass his door unless I promised to come back and marry him, but I am far too good for such as he."

" Is this really so?" cried the bailiff, who hated the miller ; " did the miller really want to marry you? If you're too good to marry him, it may be you would suit me."

" Indeed," said Kesta, " I think that might do well, for I should live in a nice house and have plenty of servants. But I have to go into the town on business, and you're sure to be somewhere about here, and when I come back we will arrange it." So she set off, leaving the bailiff chuckling at the thought of how angry the miller would be if he married Kesta.

On went Kesta in high good-humour. "Now am I indeed doing well," said she; "how clever I was not to marry Adam before I came to town." Presently she reached the town, and in the high street she passed the bank, and the banker himself stood in the doorway. He was fat and ugly and old, but his hands were covered with rings, and Kesta knew his pockets were full of gold. Kesta said, "It would be a fine thing to marry him, and I could hold up my head with any one. I think I'll speak to him, as it would be folly to pass him without trying." So she gave a loud sigh and said, "Alack a day, how hard is my lot!"

"Why, what is wrong, my pretty lass?" said the banker.

"Pretty you may well say," answered Kesta. "Would I were not so, for thence come all my troubles."

"And what are they?" asked the banker.

"Only wherever I go, I have no peace, for all the men want to marry me. First it is the farmer, then the miller, and lastly the duke's bailiff, who would scarcely let me pass on the road till I had promised him; and of course it is impossible, and I am much too pretty for any of them."

" Is this really true?" cried the banker; " if so, there must be something very superior about you. Perhaps you would be good enough for me. How would you like to be my wife, and ride in a fine carriage, and wear silk gowns all day?"

" Nay, that would be much more fitting," cried Kesta, "and from the first I thought you would be much more suitable to be my husband than any of the others I have met; but I must go down the town first, so I will come in here on my way back." So she went on till she came to a great square in front of the barracks where the soldiers were drilling, with their helmets and swords glittering in the sun, and at their head rode the General of the army. His voice was hoarse with shouting at his men, and he swore dreadfully, but he was covered with gold, and looked very grand. " Now supposing he has no wife," thought Kesta, "it would be a really fine thing to marry him : I can but try." So she waited till the soldiers were marching into the barracks, and then, when he was riding away, she went so close under the horse's feet that he shouted to her in case she should be run over. "Alas! what a life is mine," she cried very loud that he might hear, "hunted here and there till I don't know where I go!"

"Why, who hunts you?" cried the General angrily; "what nonsense you talk, my good girl."

"How dare you say I talk nonsense," cried Kesta, "when it is as much as I can do to get through your town for the men who want me to stop and marry them!"

"And why do they want you to marry them?" asked the General.

"Because I'm so pretty, of course," said Kesta promptly, and she took off her hat and looked up at the General.

"I don't think you are so pretty," he said.

"But I am," cried Kesta angrily, "and it's only stupid people who don't see it. Go and ask the men in the town. First it was a man at the farm, then the miller, then the duke's bailiff, then the banker—they all wanted to marry me, and I am much too good for any of them!"

"If this is all true," said the General, "of course you must be exceedingly pretty, and as you say you are much too good for them, perhaps

you might suit me. How would you like
that?"

"That might be better," said Kesta, "and as
you wish it very much I will agree, and I hope
you will try to make me a good husband ; but I
am obliged to go a little further on important
business, and I will meet you here on my way
back," and on she went laughing to herself.
"Indeed I am fortunate," thought she ; "and as
they all seem willing to marry me why should I
not try higher, and see what the Duke himself
would say ? There is nothing like being practical,
and it would be downright silly not to speak to the
Duke now I am here." By this time she had come
to the Duke's palace, so she stopped a servant
who was coming out and asked if he were at
home, for she said, "I have special business with
him." "He is sitting by the stream in the garden,
where he sits fishing all day, and you can go and
speak to him if you choose," said the servant.
So Kesta went through the courtyard into the
garden, and straight on to where the Duke sat
beside the stream with a long rod in his hand
fishing. He was dressed all in green, and seemed
to be half asleep, and Kesta came quite near him

before he saw her. Then she said, "Ah, pity me, your Grace, and listen to my sad story."

"Good gracious! who are you?—don't you know I am the Duke?" said he.

"And that is why I have come to you to ask you to protect me from all the men who pursue me," said Kesta.

"Why do they pursue you?" asked the Duke.

"Because I am so pretty," replied Kesta. "They all want to marry me : first the man at the farm, then the miller I met on the road, then your bailiff, then the banker, then the General of your army, and he would only let me go when I promised to go back to him."

"The General!" said the Duke. "Is this true? does he really want to marry you?"

"Of course he does," said Kesta ; "if you doubt what I say you had better send to the town and ask."

"Indeed," said the Duke, "I should not have thought you so very pretty, but if what you say is true you must be. I'm not sure if it would not suit me to marry you myself; but mind, I shall be exceedingly angry if I find you have not told me the truth, and they did not want to marry you.

Of course you would be delighted to marry me and be the Duchess?"

"Aye, that I should," cried Kesta, and she grinned with delight.

Then the Duke took from his side a horn and blew it loudly. There came from the palace four pages, dressed in blue and gold, who stood in a row to receive his orders. "See," cried the Duke, "I am going to marry this lady, who everybody thinks is very beautiful, so see that you treat her with respect; and go to the palace and bid them to prepare a feast and fitting clothes for the bride, and tell the chaplain to be ready, for I mean to marry her at once."

"And now," he said to Kesta, when all his pages had returned to the palace, "come and sit by me and watch me fish till all is ready."

So Kesta sat by his side and watched him fishing with his long rod, but after a time she grew tired of being silent, and said, "What have you caught?"

"Nothing yet," said the Duke.

"Then why do you go on?" asked she.

"Because I'm sure to catch something soon,

and it's amusing. Wouldn't you like to hold the rod a little ? "

" Yes, very much," answered Kesta, who was afraid of offending him. So she put out her hand to take the rod, and as she did so the basket fell from her arm and the cheeses rolled out.

" What are those round balls ? " asked the Duke, " and what an odd smell they have."

" They are my cheeses," cried Kesta ; " I made them yesterday, and was taking them to sell, when——"

" Good gracious, you made them ! " cried the Duke with a scream. " Then you must be a common dairy-maid, and your hands are quite rough. How terrible ! And I was just going to marry you. How dare you think yourself good enough to marry me ! " and he sprang to his feet in a towering passion, and seizing his horn blew it so loudly that the four pages ran up in great alarm. " Hunt her away," cried the Duke, " she is an impostor—a common farm wench and makes cheeses. She thought herself good enough to be the Duchess ! "

Away flew Kesta, with the pages after her hooting and shouting, " Down with the imperti-

nent hussy who wanted to marry the Duke, a
common dairy-maid who makes cheeses."

On rushed Kesta till she came to the General's
house, and at his window he sat in his fine
uniform. He sat waiting for her, but when he
saw the pages behind her he called, "Hey-dey,
what is all this fuss about?"

"It is nothing," said Kesta. "See, I have
come back to marry you as I promised."

But here the pages shouted, "Away with the
impertinent dairy-maid, who thought herself good
enough to marry the Duke."

"And wouldn't the Duke marry her?" asked
the General.

"Of course not; she is nothing but a farm
wench," cried the pages, "and she is to be chased
from the town for her impertinence."

"And so she shall," cried the General; "she
thought she was fit for me too—it is disgraceful!"
and he cried to some soldiers who stood by his
door, "Here, my men, help to chase this good-
for-nothing hussy out of the town."

But before he had finished Kesta was running
down the street with all her might to the
banker's. At last she came to the banker's big

square house standing beside the bank, and on the steps was the banker himself in his shiny black clothes with gold rings on his hands.

"Here I am," cried Kesta; "and let me in quickly, for I am out of breath with running."

"Why have you hurried so?" cried the banker, and as he spoke the pages and the soldiers came round the corner, "and what is all this shouting for?"

"Nay, how should I know?" cried Kesta, running into the house.

But up came her pursuers, crying, "Away with her! down with her!"

"Who is it you are calling after?" asked the banker.

"That wench in the yellow dress who has gone into your house."

"Why, what has she done?" he asked.

"Why, she thought herself good enough to marry the Duke and the General, and she is to be hooted out of the town for her impudence!"

"But didn't the General want to marry her?" asked the banker.

"Our General!" cried the soldiers angrily; "why, she's only a dairy-maid, and not fit for him."

" Then I'm sure she can't be good enough for me, for I'm quite as good as he," said the banker, and he ran into the house in a great rage, crying, " Begone, you impertinent jade! how dare you think yourself good enough for me to marry!" It chanced at this moment that the clerks were coming out of the bank next door, and when he saw them he cried, " Here, my good fellows, help to chase this minx from the town ; she wishes to be my wife, when she is nothing but a common dairy-maid." On this the clerks burst out laughing, and one and all ran after Kesta, who ran with all her might and main.

" It's too hard," sobbed she ; " what have I done to be treated like this?" But run as fast as she might she could not reach the bailiff's house before them, and the pages, soldiers, and clerks were all close to her, shouting and laughing.

"Why, what's the matter?" cried the bailiff, "and why are you shouting at this poor maid?"

" Why," said they, " she wanted to marry first the Duke, and the General, and the banker, and of course they would not have her, because she is only a common dairy wench."

" What impertinence!" cried the bailiff; "and,

now I come to think of it, she asked to marry
me too ; indeed she merits punishment for such
behaviour," and seeing some of his farm people
close at hand, he bid them run after Kesta and
drive her out of the town. But this time she had
started first, and had got on to the mill before they
could reach her, and she ran into the garden where
the miller was. "Well, I'm glad to see you back,"
said he, " but how hard you have run."

" I was in such a hurry to get back. Now let's
go into the house," she said.

"Come along," said the miller ; "but what
are all those people shouting for ? "

" 'Tis only the farmers bringing home pigs
from the market," said Kesta, but she felt frightened, for she heard the people calling after
her.

" Pigs don't make a noise like that," said the
miller, " I will go and see what it is about." And
when he heard that they were all shouting at
Kesta, he flew into a violent rage and cried, " If
she wasn't good enough for the bailiff I'm sure
she's not fit for me," and he called to some of his
men who were working at the mill, " See there,
my men, do you see that girl ? throw some flour

E

at her, for she is an impudent hussy, and asked
me to marry her."

Away flew Kesta again, and after her came all
the crowd in a long line. "How unfortunate I
am," she sobbed; "but anyhow I can go back to
Adam; he's sure to be glad to have me," and on
she sped, and at last she came to the farm and
ran in, calling to Adam.

"Is that you, Kesta?" cried Adam, coming to
meet her, and kissing her. "I'm glad to see you,
but why are you so hot?"

"It is the sun, it was so strong," said Kesta.

"Then sit down and grow cool," said Adam.
"But I wonder what all that shouting outside
can be?"

"It is only people making holiday," cried
Kesta. But for all she could say Adam went out
to ask the people what they wanted at the farm?

"We want nothing at the farm," they cried,
"but we followed that impudent wench dressed
in yellow."

"Why, what has she done?" asked Adam.

"Done!" they cried. "Why, she came up to
the town and asked to marry the miller, and the
banker, and the bailiff, and the General, and even

the Duke himself, so she deserves to be punished for her presumption."

Then Adam looked very grave, and went back to the farm and said, "Indeed, Kesta, I cannot marry you now, since you've been to the town and tried to get a finer husband than me," and he went back to his work, and left Kesta sitting all alone; and there she sat and cried by herself, and did not get any husband after all, because she was so false and vain.

THE POOL & THE TREE

NCE there was a tree standing in the middle of a vast wilderness, and beneath the shade of its branches was a little pool, over which they bent. The pool looked up at the tree and the tree looked down at the pool, and the two loved each other better than anything else on earth. And neither of them thought of anything else but each other, or cared who came and went in the world around them.

"But for you and the shade you give me I should have been dried up by the sun long ago," said the pool.

52

"And if it were not for you and your shining face, I should never have seen myself, or have known what my boughs and blossoms were like," answered the tree.

Every year when the leaves and flowers had died away from the branches of the tree, and the cold winter came, the little pool froze over and remained hard and silent till the spring; but directly the sun's rays thawed it, it again sparkled and danced as the wind blew upon it, and it began to watch its beloved friend, to see the buds and leaves reappear, and together they counted the leaves and blossoms as they came forth.

One day there rode over the moorland a couple of travellers in search of rare plants and flowers. At first they did not look at the tree, but as they were hot and tired they got off their horses, and sat under the shade of the boughs, and talked of what they had been doing. "We have not found much," said one gloomily; "it seemed scarcely worth while to come so far for so little."

"One may hunt for many years before one finds anything very rare," answered the elder traveller. "Well, we have not done, and who knows but what we may yet have some luck?" As he spoke he picked up one of the fallen leaves of the tree which lay beside him, and at once he sprang to his feet, and pulled down one of the branches to examine it. Then he called to his comrade to get up, and he also closely examined the leaves and blossoms, and they talked together eagerly, and at length declared that this was the best thing they had found in all their travels. But neither the pool nor the tree heeded them, for the pool lay looking lovingly up to the tree, and the tree gazed down at the clear water of the pool, and they wanted nothing more, and by and by the travellers mounted their horses and rode away.

The summer passed and the cold winds of autumn blew.

"Soon your leaves will drop and you will fall asleep for the winter, and we must bid each other good-bye," said the pool.

"And you too when the frost comes will be numbed to ice," answered the tree; "but never mind, the spring will follow, and the sun will wake us both."

But long before the winter had set in, ere yet the last leaf had fallen, there came across the prairie a number of men riding on horses and mules, bringing with them a long waggon. They rode straight to the tree, and foremost among them were the two travellers who had been there before.

"Why do they come? What do they want?" cried the pool uneasily; but the tree feared nothing. The men had spades and pickaxes, and began to dig a deep ditch all round the tree's roots, and then they dug beneath them, and at last both the pool and the tree saw that they were going to dig it up.

"What are you doing? Why are you trying to wrench up my roots and to move me?" cried the tree; "don't you know that I shall die if you drag me from my pool which has fed and loved me all my life?" And the pool said, "Oh, what can they want? Why do they take you? The sun will come and dry me up without your shade, and I never, never shall see you again." But the men heard nothing, and continued to dig at the root of the tree till they had loosened all the earth round it, and then they lifted it and wrapped big

cloths round it and put it on their waggon and
drove away with it.

Then for the first time the pool looked straight
up at the sky without seeing the delicate tracery
made by the leaves and twigs against the blue,
and it called out to all things near it: " My tree,
my tree, where have they taken my tree? When
the hot sun comes it will dry me up, if it shines
down on me without the shade of my tree." And
so loudly it mourned and lamented that the birds
flying past heard it, and at last a swallow paused
on the wing, and hovering near its surface, asked
why it grieved so bitterly. " They have taken
my tree," cried the pool, "and I don't know where
it is ; I cannot move or look to right or left, so I
shall never see it again."

"Ask the moon," said the swallow. " The
moon sees everywhere, and she will tell you. I
am flying away to warmer countries, for the winter
will soon be here. Good-bye, poor pool."

At night, when the moon rose, and the pool
looked up and saw its beautiful white face, it
remembered the swallow's words, and called out
to ask its aid.

" Find me my tree," it prayed; "you shone

through its branches and know it well, and you can see all over the world; look for my tree, and tell me where they have taken it. Perhaps they have torn it in pieces or burnt it up."

"Nay," cried the moon, "they have done neither, for I saw it a few hours ago when I shone near it. They have taken it many miles away and it is planted in a big garden, but it has not taken root in the earth, and its foliage is fading. The men who took it prize it heartily, and strangers come from far and near to look at it, because they say it is so rare, and there are only one or two like it in the world."

On hearing this the pool felt itself swell with pride that the tree should be so much admired; but then it cried in anguish, "And I shall never see it again, for I can never move from here."

"That is nonsense," cried a little cloud that was sailing near; "I was once in the earth like you. To-morrow, if the sun shines brightly, he will draw you up into the sky, and you can sail along till you find your tree."

"Is that true?" cried the pool, and all that night it rested in peace waiting for the sun to rise. Next day there were no clouds, and when the

pool saw the sun shining it cried, " Draw me up
into the sky, dear Sun, that I may be a little cloud
and sail all the world over, till I can find my
beloved tree."

When the sun heard it, he threw down hundreds
of tiny golden threads which dropped over the
pool, and slowly and gradually it began to change
and grow thinner and lighter, and to rise through
the air, till at last it had quite left the earth, and
where it had lain before, there was nothing but a
dry hole, but the pool itself was transformed into
a tiny cloud, and was sailing above in the blue
sky in the sunshine. There were many other
little clouds in the sky, but our little cloud kept
apart from them all. It could see far and near
over a great space of country, but nowhere could
it espy the tree, and again it turned to the sun for
help. " Can you see ? " it cried. " You who see
everywhere, where is my tree ? "

" You can't see it yet," answered the sun, " for
it is away on the other side of the world, but
presently the wind will begin to blow and it will
blow you till you find it."

Then the wind arose, and the cloud sailed along
swiftly, looking everywhere as it went for the tree.

It could have had a merry time if it had not longed so for its friend. Everywhere was the golden sunlight shining through the bright blue sky, and the other clouds tumbled and danced in the wind and laughed for joy.

"Why do you not come and dance with us?" they cried; "why do you sail on so rapidly?"

"I cannot stay, I am seeking a lost friend," answered the cloud, and it scudded past them, leaving them to roll over and over, and tumble about, and change their shapes, and divide and separate, and play a thousand pranks.

For many hundred miles the wind blew the little cloud, then it said, "Now I am tired and shall take you no further, but soon the west wind will come and it will take you on; good-bye." And at once the wind stopped blowing and dropped to rest on the earth; and the cloud stood still in the sky and looked all around.

"I shall never find it," it sighed. "It will be dead before I come."

Presently the sun went down and the moon rose, then the west wind began to blow gently and moved the cloud slowly along.

"Which way should I go, where is it?" entreated the cloud.

"I know; I will take you straight to it," said the west wind. "The north wind has told me. I blew by the tree to-day; it was drooping, but when I told it that you had risen to the sky and were seeking it, it revived and tried to lift its branches. They have planted it in a great garden, and there are railings round it and no one may touch it; and there is one gardener who has nothing to do but to attend to it, and people come from far and near to look at it because it is so rare, and they have only found one or two others like it, but it longs to be back in the desert, stooping over you and seeing its face in your water."

"Make haste, then," cried the cloud, "lest before I reach it I fall to pieces with joy at the thought of seeing it."

"How foolish you are!" said the wind. "Why should you give yourself up for a tree? You might dance about in the sky for long yet, and then you might drop into the sea and mix with the waves and rise again with them to the sky, but if you fall about the tree you will go straight into the dark earth, and perhaps you will always

" Have you come at last ? " the Tree cried ; " then we need never be parted again.'

remain there, for at the roots of the tree they have made a deep hole and the sun cannot draw you up through the earth under the branches."

" Then that will be what I long for," cried the cloud. " For then I can lie in the dark where no one may see me, but I shall be close to my tree, and I can touch its roots and feed them, and when the raindrops fall from its branches they will run down to me and tell me how they look."

" You are foolish," said the wind again ; " but you shall have what you want."

The wind blew the cloud low down near the earth till it found itself over a big garden, in which there were all sorts of trees and shrubs, and such soft green grass as the cloud had never seen before. And there in the middle of the grass, in a bed of earth to itself, with a railing round it so that no one could injure it, was the tree which the cloud had come so far to seek. Its leaves were falling off, its branches were drooping, and its buds dropped before they opened, and the poor tree looked as if it were dying.

" There is my tree, my tree ! " called the cloud.

" Blow me down, dear wind, so that I may fall upon it."

The wind blew the cloud lower and lower, till it almost touched the top branches of the tree. Then it broke and fell in a shower, and crept down through the earth to its roots, and when it felt its drops the tree lifted up its leaves and rejoiced, for it knew that the pool it had loved so had followed it.

" Have you come at last?" it cried. " Then we need never be parted again."

In the morning when the gardeners came they found the tree looking quite fresh and well, and its leaves quite green and crisp. " The cool wind last night revived it," they said, "and it looks as if it had rained too in the night, for round here the earth is quite damp." But they did not know that under the earth at the tree's roots lay the pool, and that that was what had saved the tree.

And there it lies to this day, hidden away in the darkness where no one can see it, but the tree feels it with its roots, and blooms in splendour, and people come from far and near to admire it.

NCE there lived a young girl called Nanina, who kept sheep for an old far-mer. One day he said to her, " Nanina, I'm going away to buy pigs at a market far off, and I shall be away one whole month, so be sure and take good care of the flock, and re-member, there are six sheep and eight lambs, and I must find them safe when I return.

And mind, Nanina, that whatever you do, you
don't go near the old palace on the other side of
the hill, for it is filled with wicked fairies who
might do you an ill turn." Nanina promised,
and her master started.

The first day all went well, and she drove the
flock in safely at night ; but the next day she
found it dull sitting on the hillside watching the
lambs at play, and wondered why her master had
told her always to keep on that side, and away
from the old palace on the other.

" If it is filled with fairies," quoth she, "it won't
hurt me just to look at it ; I should like to see a
fairy." So she drove her flock to the other side
of the hill, and sat looking at the old palace that
was half in ruins, but was said to be lit up quite
brightly every night after it was dark.

" I wonder if it really is lit up," said Nanina,
"I should like to see." So she waited on that side
of the hill till the sun went down, and then she
saw a bright light appearing in one of the palace
windows. As she stood and watched, the front
door opened, and out there came a shepherd boy
followed by a flock of black goats. Nanina
stared at him, for she had never seen any one so

beautiful before. He was dressed in glittering green, and wore a soft brown hat trimmed with leaves under which his curls hung down. In one hand he held a crook and in the other a pipe, and as he drew near, he began to play the pipe and dance merrily, while the goats behind him skipped and danced too. Nanina had never seen such goats ; they were jet black, with locks curling and thick and soft as silk. As she listened open-mouthed to the music of the pipe, she heard it speak words in its playing :—

> " When the young birds sing,
> And the young plants spring,
> Then dance we so merrily together, oh."

The shepherd boy danced lightly to where she stood, and louder and louder sounded the pipe, and still it said—

> " When the young birds sing,
> And the young plants spring,
> Then dance we so merrily together, oh."

Nanina gaped to see the goats dance and spring in time to the music, and so cheering it was, that she felt her own feet beginning to move with it. The shepherd made her a low bow and offered

her his hand, and she placed hers in it, and off they
started together. Nanina's feet felt as light as
if they had been made of cork, and she laughed
with glee as she bounded on ; and as she danced
with the shepherd, so her flock began to move
too, and thus they went, followed by the black
goats and sheep all skipping merrily. " If my
flock follow me there can be no harm," thought
Nanina, and on they kept in time to the wonderful
tune—

> " When the young birds sing,
> And the young plants spring,
> Then dance we so merrily together, oh."

Whither they went she knew not, she thought
of nothing but the joy of dancing to the wonderful
music; but suddenly, just ere sunrise, the shepherd
stopped, and dropped her hand and gave one
long slow note on the pipe, at which the goats
gathered round him, and before she knew where
they were going, they had disappeared into the
palace. Then she was in a terrible fright, for she
saw the sun beginning to rise, and found the
whole night had passed, when she thought she
had only been ten minutes. She counted her
sheep, and, alas! there was one lamb missing.

She sought everywhere for it, but no trace of it
was to be seen. Then she drove all the others

back to the farm and watched them, falling half
asleep, for she was weary with the dancing. But

when evening came, and she had slept some time, she said to herself, " Surely the best plan would be to go back to the old palace, and see if I can see the shepherd and the black goats again." So just about sunset she returned to the palace, and again the door opened, and the beautiful shepherd boy came out with the black goats following. But when he began to play on his pipe, and the goats to dance, Nanina forgot all about the lost lamb and danced with him as before. Again they danced till morning, and then he left her suddenly, and she found that another lamb had disappeared. Then she wept and lamented, and declared that the next night she would only watch the shepherd and nothing would make her dance ; and again the next night the same thing happened ; when once she heard the pipe, Nanina could not keep still, and another lamb was lost. This went on to the end of a fortnight, when there was only one of the flock left. Then she was terribly frightened, for her master would soon return, and she did not know what she should say to him. But still she went back and sat by the old palace, and when the shepherd came out, and she heard the music, she

could not refrain from dancing, and in the morning
the last lamb had gone!

All the day Nanina wandered about and cried,
but no sheep were to be found. At last, when

she was quite weary, she sat down beneath a beech
tree near the palace, and leaned her head against
its trunk sobbing.   Then she saw that someone
had torn down the lowest branches of the tree
and they were hanging down broken.   She raised
them and tied them up, so that they would grow
together, and as she did so she heard a shadowy
voice whisper, "Thank you, Nanina; Nanina, don't
dance."   She looked about but there was nobody
there, and again she heard a whisper, " Nanina,
don't dance."   The voice came from the beech
tree, and among the leaves she saw a small twisted
face looking at her.   " Thank you, Nanina, for
saving my bough," said the tree, "and if you mind
me, you shall get all your sheep back again."

" My sheep," cried Nanina.   " Only tell me,
and I will do anything."

" Then you must not dance.   Every time you
refuse to dance with the fairy, one of your flock
will be returned."

" But how can I refuse to dance?" cried Nanina,
"for as I hear the pipe beginning, my feet begin
to move of themselves, it is no use my trying,"
and she cried aloud.

" Bury your feet in the earth like my roots,"

whispered back the voice. "Dig a hole deep down, and I will hold your feet so that you shall not move them, only you must bear the pain, and not mind if you walk lame afterwards, for I shall hold them very tight, and it will hurt you."

"Hurt me as you please," cried Nanina, "and I shan't mind. If only I can get back my sheep I will bear any pain." So she knelt beneath the tree, and dug a deep hole in the ground among its roots, and then she placed her feet among the loose earth, and she felt something moving near them which tightened around and drew them far down into the ground, and held them as if they were bound with cords. She saw the lights in the windows of the palace, and the door opened. "Hold me, hold me fast," she cried, "for when I hear the music I shall begin to dance." The tree said nothing, but she felt its roots tightening so that she could not move. The door of the palace opened as before, and the beautiful shepherd, followed by his goats and her sheep, came out, and she heard once more the sound of the wonderful pipe, and he danced straight up to the tree beneath which she stood, and held out his hand to her. Nanina felt as if her feet were beginning

to move under the earth, but the roots of the
tree held them so firmly that she could not stir
one inch. Still the shepherd danced before her,
and as she saw him springing in front, with
the flocks behind him following him, she grew
quite wild to dance, and tried her hardest to
break her feet free from the roots which held

them, but in vain, though she almost screamed
with the pain they cost her. For hours the
shepherd danced in front of her, till, as before,
the pipe sounded forth one long note, and he
disappeared, but this time not all the flock went
with him, for beside her was left one of her
own little lambs, and when she saw it she cried

for joy. She felt the roots releasing their hold of her feet, and she drew them out of the earth, and they were all blue and bruised where they had been held. She drove home the lamb and fastened it into the sheep-pen, but her feet were so stiff and swelled that she limped as she walked. Next night she went back to the beech tree, and again slipped her feet into its roots, and felt them twist around them ; but this time the poor feet were so sore that she cried when they touched them. Again the fairy appeared, and again she heard the pipe, and her longing to dance was worse than ever, but the roots clutched her and would not let her stir. When the pipe ceased and the fairy disappeared, another of her lambs was left with her, and she drove it home as she had done the first, but she had to go very slowly on account of her crushed feet.

The same thing happened the next night and the next, till all the flock had returned save one, and Nanina's feet were so bad that she could scarcely hobble, for they were crushed and bleeding, and she wondered whether she would walk lame all the days of her life.

On the last evening she limped down to the

tree almost crying with pain. When she sat
down by its trunk she heard the soft sighing
voice saying, " Never mind, Nanina ; to-night
is the last, and though it will hurt you the
most, it will soon be past." So she slipped her
feet into the earth once more, though she shrank
as they touched it, and directly the sun had
set, the lights appeared in the palace windows,
and out came the shepherd with all his black
goats and her one white sheep following him.
He looked more beautiful than ever, for he had a
crown set with jewels, and was dressed in scarlet
and gold, but when the pipe began to play it was
not merry dance-music it made, but long sad
notes, like a funeral march ; yet Nanina's feet
would have moved in spite of herself, and she
would have marched in time to them, had not the
roots tightened like cords and held her down.
Tears of pain ran down her cheeks, and she
sobbed, and instead of the joyous words what the
music said was—

> " Join us, Nanina, dance again,
>   One last dance will ease your pain."

Presently the music grew quicker, and her long-

"Join us, Nanina, dance again,
One last dance will ease your pain."

ing to move with it grew stronger. She swayed
herself about, and cried and screamed as the fairy
and flock danced, now solemnly and slowly, now
joyously and wildly. Just when she felt that she
could bear it no longer there came one long low
note on the pipe, and with a mighty crash like
thunder the shepherd and the goats disappeared,
and not only had they gone, but the walls of the
old palace had fallen, and nothing was left of it
but a heap of stones. Beside her on the grass
was the last of her lost sheep. " Good-bye,
Nanina," said the voice from the beech tree;
" now you have all your flock again," and she felt
the roots loosen round her feet, but when she
looked at them she found that her legs were
wounded and bleeding, where she had dashed
them about in trying to dance. She knelt down
and smoothed over the earth where it was torn up
among the trees, and she put her arms round the
trunk and kissed and thanked it for having helped
her, but the voice did not speak again. Then she
drove home the last sheep, but she had to go on
her hands and knees, for her feet were too bad to
walk.

Next day when the farmer came home, he was

well pleased that she had kept his flock safe, but he would fain know how she had got such sore feet that for long she must walk lame. "Of a truth, master," she quoth, "it was in saving the lambs when they got into dangerous places."

Underneath the beech tree, where Nanina's feet had bled among the earth, there sprang up pretty little scarlet flowers, and whenever she passed and saw them she remembered how she had been punished for disobeying her master, and made up her mind never to do so again.

THE END

IN a little village there lived a young potter, who made his living by making all sorts of earthenware. He took the clay, and made it into shapes on the wheel, and then baked his cups and jars in a kiln. He made big jugs and little jugs, and basins and cups and saucers, and indeed every sort of pot or jar that could be wanted. He was very fond of his work, and was always thinking of how to make new shapes, or colour his jars with pretty colours. It was a very tiny village he lived in, and he worked at throwing his pots

81   G

on his wheel by the roadside, but people came from many other villages and towns to buy his ware. Once a year there was a big fair, held in the town near, and just before it, the potter was always very busy making new pots and jugs to sell there. A few nights before the fair was to be held, he was hard at work, trying to finish a number of little bowls, so he sat at his wheel late in the evening after the sun was set. All day long the road had been gay with folk coming to the fair, some were in carts, and some were on foot, and there were a number of gipsies in caravans, bringing all sorts of goods to sell. Most of them went through the village and on to a big common a little further on, where they got out of their carts and put up tents, to sleep in while the fair went on. The potter was so busy with his little basins on his turning wheel that he did not hear the sound of footsteps, and when he looked up, he was surprised to see a young gipsy girl standing near, watching him. She was quite young, and had big black eyes, and rosy round cheeks, and her black hair was twisted up in little red beads and chains. She was dressed in some very gay stuff, and round her neck was a gold necklace, and on her fingers and arms were rings and bracelets.

"That should be a fine cup," said the girl, "since you keep your eyes on it and can look at nothing else."

"I keep my eyes for my work, that I may do it well," said the potter, "for I live by my work, and neither by stealing nor begging."

"But I fancy many others can do your work as well, or better than you," answered the gipsy. "What can your cups do when they are finished? I don't hear you say anything to them, so I should think they would be stupid cups—only fit to drink out of."

"And what else should they be for?" asked the potter angrily. "What do you mean by saying that you don't hear me saying anything to my cups? I don't think you know what you are talking about. It is nonsense, and you are talking nonsense."

"My grandfather used to make pots on a wheel," said the gipsy, and she laughed low, and showed her white teeth in the moonlight; "ah! but he knew how to do them, and he had charms to say to them when he threw them. And one of his cups would make you wise if you drank out of it, and another would give you your true love's heart if she drank from it, and another would make you forget everything—yes, even your true love, and all your mirth and all your sorrow, and I think that was the best cup of all ; " and again the gipsy laughed in the moonlight, and sang a little song to herself as she sat herself down before the potter.

" Now this is real child's talk," said the potter very impatiently. " 'Tis easy to say your grandfather knew how to do all this, but why should I believe you ? and because your grandfather may have been able to throw a bowl upon the wheel, that doesn't make you know anything about the craft, or how it is done."

" Nay, but he taught me too," said the gipsy. " Give me a piece of your clay, and let me come to your wheel and you shall see."

At first the potter thought she was talking nonsense, but to his great surprise she took hold of the clay in her little brown hands, and moulded and modelled it with the greatest skill. Then she placed it on the wheel and threw a little jug, and he wondered to see how deft she was.

" Now I will make you a little bowl," she said,
and then she made jugs and pots and jars, far
more quickly and skilfully than the potter could
have done. "And now I will colour them too,"
she cried. " See, I shall catch the colour from the
moon, and to-morrow you can put them into your
kiln and bake them, and you may be sure that
you have never had such pots there before."
Then she put her little brown hands out into the
moonlight, and they were covered with rings
which glittered and shone, but as she held up her
palms to the moon's rays, it seemed to the potter as
if they too were full of some strange glittering
liquid. " And now," she said, " see, I will put it
on to your pots, and I should think I had taught
you that I know more about your trade than you
do yourself." And she took the pots in her hands
and rubbed her palms over them, and she traced
patterns on them with her fingers.

The potter looked at her and felt almost angry,
but she only laughed in his face.

" And now one last thing," she cried, "and
that is, that I will make you a cup that has a spell
in it, and it shall be a present for you to remember me by. It will be very plain, and there

will be no gay colours in it, but when you give it to
your true love to drink from, if once you have
drunk from it yourself, you will have all her heart,
but beware that she doesn't take a second draught.
For though the first draught that she drinks will
be drunk to love, the second draught will be drunk
to hate, and though she have loved you more
than all else on earth, all her love will turn to hate
when she drinks again.   And as you are so
ignorant how to make bowls and cups, you will
not know how to fashion one so as to win back
her love again."

The potter stared in silence, while the gipsy
took another bit of clay and placed it upon the
wheel, and then she bent her head, which glittered
with beads and coins, low over it, and placing her
rosy lips close to the mouth of the cup, sang some
words into it, while she moulded it with her hands,
and turned the wheel with her foot.   It was in
some strange language that the potter had never
heard before.

"Good-bye," she said presently.   " Now, there,
that is for you, and be sure you do not sell the
little brown cup, but keep it and give it to your
true love to drink out of ; but only one draught, for

if there are two maybe you will need the gipsy's help again." Then she laughed, and nodding her head over her shoulder, tripped lightly away in the moonlight while the potter stared after her.

At first he thought he had been asleep, but there around him stood the little rows of jugs and pots which the gipsy had made, and truly they were beautifully done. He took them up, and turned them over in his hand, and wondered at their shape and workmanship.

"To-morrow," he said, "I will put them into the kiln, and see how they come out. She certainly was a clever wench, and knew her work ; but as for her talk about having coloured them, that was all nonsense, and as for breathing spells and charms into the cups, why it is like baby's talk."

But next day when the pots were baked, the potter was even more surprised, for they had the most wonderful colours that he had ever seen : silver, blue, grey and yellow, in all sorts of patterns, all save the little brown cup, which was the last the gipsy had made. But when he looked at it the potter felt a little uncomfortable, and began to wonder if it really did contain the charm as she had declared.

When the fair began, the potter placed all the gipsy's wares on a stall with his own, and marked them with very high prices, but had he asked three times as much he could have got it, for there were some rich folk from the big houses who came to the fair, and they at once bought them all up, declaring that such pots and jugs they had never seen. At this the potter was well pleased, and found that he had made more money than he had earned in many a long month past; but when people wanted him to make them more like them, he was obliged to shake his head, and say, " That he was very sorry, but he had had them coloured from afar, and he did not know where he could now have them done." Of the gipsy he saw nothing more, though he looked for her everywhere during the three days in which the fair lasted, but she was not to be seen, and when the fair was over, and the other people were packing their carts and vans to go on their way, he saw very many gipsies, and supposed that she had gone with some of them, without giving him the chance of speaking to her again.

Years went by, and the potter never heard
anything more of the gipsy, indeed he would have
thought it had all been a dream if it had not been
for the little brown pot standing on the shelf.
Sometimes he took it up, and looked at it, and
wondered when he saw how well and cleverly it
was made. He still laughed when he remembered
what the gipsy had said about leaving a charm
in it, for though he himself had drunk out of it
many times, he never thought it had brought any
spell on him.

One year when the fair was being held, the
potter was at his place as usual with his stall
covered with pots, and there came and placed
herself beside him at the next stall a woman
with some spinning-wheels. Her stall was
covered with fine linen cloths woven in pretty
patterns, and so fine and well wrought were they,
that many people wanted to buy them. With her
were her two daughters, and one sat at the
spinning-wheel and spun the flax, and the other
had a hand-loom and wove it when it was spun
to show the good folk how the cloths were made.
Both were pretty girls, but the girl who had the
hand-loom had the sweetest face the potter had

ever seen. Her eyes were very blue, and her hair was like golden corn, and when she smiled, it was as if the sun shone. The potter watched her as she sat weaving, and could not keep his eyes from her or attend properly to his own pots, or to the people who wanted to buy them. Every day he watched the young girl at her work, for the fair lasted for a week, and the more he looked at her the more he wanted to look, till at last he said to himself that somehow or other he must get her for his wife ; so when the fair was done he begged her to marry him, and to remain with him, and he said he would always work for her, and she should want for nothing. The mother was a poor widow, and she and her daughters made their bread by going about the country spinning and weaving, and she would have been quite willing that the potter should marry her daughter, but the girl only laughed, and said that she scarcely knew the potter, but when she came back again the next year to the fair, she would give him his answer. So the widow and her two daughters went away, and no sign of them was left with the potter, save a lock of golden hair, which he had begged from the daughter.

The year passed away, but to the potter it seemed the longest year he had ever lived. He pined for the time to come when the fair should be held, and the widow and her daughters should return. As the time drew near he got down the brown cup, and looked at it again and again. " Nay," he said, " what harm could it do ? the gipsy said it would give me my true love's heart if she drank out of it after I had drunk, and I have drunk out of it many a time. I don't believe it, but all the same it would be no harm for her to drink from it."

And so when the fair was opened, he took the brown cup down with him, and stood it upon the stall with his other ware. The spinning woman and her two daughters came back with their fine cloths, and their wheel and their loom, and when he saw the golden-haired girl, he loved her still more than before, for he thought her eyes were bluer and her smile was brighter. He watched her all the time as she sat weaving, but said nothing, but when the fair was over, and they were packing their goods to go on their way, he pressed the maid for her answer. Still she hesitated, and then the potter took the little

brown cup off his stall, and poured into it some
choice wine, and said to her,

"If then you wish to go away, and never see me
again, I pray you drink one draught, in remembrance of the happy days we have had together."

The young girl took the cup, but no sooner had
she tasted it than she put it down and turned her
eyes on the potter, and said in a low voice,

"I will stay with you always, if you want me,
and will be a true wife to you, and love you better
than anything on earth."

So the potter married her, and she went to live
in his little cottage.

Time passed, and the potter and his young wife
lived together very happily, and every day he
thought her fairer and sweeter. And they had
a little baby girl with blue eyes like its mother's,
and the potter thought himself the happiest man on
earth, and the little brown pot stood on the shelf,
and the potter looked at it, and still he would not
believe about the charm, for he said to himself,
"My wife loved me for my own sake, and not for
any silly charm or nonsense."

So for a time all things went well, but there came
a day when the potter had to go to a neighbouring

"I pray you drink one draught, in remembrance of the happy days we
have had together."

town and leave his wife at home alone all day. When he was gone she sat by the window with her little child, and presently there came up outside a dark, rough - looking man, with a wicked face, and he looked at her as she sat rocking the cradle, and thought she was the most beautiful woman he had ever seen on earth. When he looked at her the potter's wife was frightened, but when he told her he was very hungry, and begged her for food and drink, she rose, for her heart was tender, and she fetched him bread and meat, and spread them on the table before him. So the rough man came into the cottage and sat at the table, and ate the potter's bread and meat, and drank his wine. "And who is your husband, and where is he?" he said. "I am sure he is a lucky man to have such a wife and such a home."

"Yes, truly," said the potter's wife. "We are very happy, and we love each other dearly, and we really have nothing else to wish for."

Then the gipsy man said, "But your dress is plain, and your rooms are bare; now, were you the wife of some wealthy man, he would give you pearls and diamonds for your neck, and beautiful silks and satins."

" No, but I don't want them," said the potter's wife smiling. " My husband works very hard, and he gives me all he can, and I am quite content with it."

" And you say he is a potter ; then what sort of things does he make ? " asked the gipsy man as he cast his eyes about the room, and they lit upon the little brown jug standing upon the shelf. " And did he make the little bowl there ? "

" I don't know," said his wife, and she took it down and turned it about in her hand. " I suppose so, but he has told me it was very old."

The gipsy man seized it eagerly, and poured wine in it, and looked inside it, and then he laughed, and stooping his head over it, said a few words, and then laughed again.

" I have seen cups like this before," he said. " And they are worth a mint of money, though you would not think it. And have you never drunk out of it ? Has it not been used ? "

" I don't drink from it," said the potter's wife, " but I believe I did so once, and that was on the day when I promised my husband I would be his wife."

Then the gipsy laughed again and again. "See," he said, "I am going a long way off, perhaps to die by cold and hunger by the roadside, while you and your husband are cosy and warm. You set small store by this cup, but it may be that in foreign countries I could sell it for what would keep me for many a long day. Give it to me, I pray you, that I may take it with me."

The potter's wife hesitated and trembled. She was afraid of the man, and she thought he had a hard, bad face, but she did not want to seem unkind.

" Well, take it," she said ; " but why should you want it ? "

Then the gipsy man came and caught her by the arm. " Now," he said, " you are the fairest woman I have ever seen, and I am going away, and shall never see you again. So I beg you wish me God-speed, and drink my health out of the little brown cup you have given me. And if your lips have touched it, it will be the dearest thing I have on earth ! "

H

Then the potter's wife was still more frightened, and trembled more than before. But the man looked so dark and threatening, that she did not like to refuse him, and she took the cup in her hand.

"And then you will go on your way," she said.

"And then I shall go on my way," cried the gipsy. "And you will wait here till your husband comes, whom you love more than anything else on this earth."

Then the potter's wife bent her head and tasted the wine out of the cup, and wished the gipsy happiness. And when she had done so he laughed again, long and low, till her heart sank with fear, and he picked up the cup and put it into his bundle, and went his way. Then the potter's wife sat down by the cradle, and almost cried, she knew not why, and the whole room seemed cold, and when she looked out at the sunshine it looked dark, and she bent over the baby in the cradle with her tears falling.

"Alack!" she cried, "why doesn't my husband come home? Where is he gone? How cruel it is to leave me all alone here, so that any rough man may come into the house. In truth I don't think he can love me much, since all he thinks of is to go away and leave me; and as for me, surely I could have had many a better husband, and one who should have loved me more. How foolish I was to marry him."

Thus she sat and lamented all day, and in the evening, when the potter drove up to his door and cried out "Wife, wife," she wouldn't go out to receive him. And when he came in to their little sitting-room, he found her with tears in her eyes, sitting lamenting and complaining. When he went up to her to take her in his arms and kiss her, she turned away from him and would not let him touch her, and the potter, who had never seen his wife cross or angry, knew that there must be something wrong. She must be ill, he thought; to-morrow or the next day she will be well again. So he urged her to rest well, and took no notice of her angry words; but the next day, and the next, there was no change, and things were growing from bad to worse. For now the wife wouldn't speak to him at all, and when she came nigh him she looked at him with anger, and would not even suffer him to touch the hem of her dress. Then the potter began

to think of the little brown cup, and he looked
up at the shelf and saw that it was not there,
and he began to feel very much alarmed.

"Why," he said, "what has become of my
little old brown cup that used to stand up on
the shelf?"

"I gave it to a gipsy man," she answered
scornfully. "He seemed to like it, and I didn't
see that I was obliged to keep all the rubbish
that you had in the house."

Then the potter groaned within himself and
said,

"But did you just take it off the shelf and give
it to him, and did he ask you for it? Why did
he want it?"

"Of course he asked for it," said the wife very
angrily, "and I just gave it him when I had drunk
his health out of it, as he wished me to."

Then the potter was stricken with deadly fear,
and remembered the words of the gipsy. "The
first draught she will drink to your love, and the
second draught she will drink to your hate," and
he knew in his heart that the words were true,
and that the cup carried with it a charm.

He sat and thought and thought, and waited

many days, hoping that his wife would change, and love him as before, but she remained cold and hard. Then the potter packed a wallet full of clothes, and put some money in his pocket, and he went to his wife and said,

" Wife, there is a man somewhere who has done me a great wrong, and perhaps he did it unwittingly. I am going out to find him, and to make him right it, and though you do not love me, you will bide here quietly with your baby till I come back. And I do not know if that will be

in months or in years." Then the potter's wife fell a-crying.

" I do not love you, nay, I hate you, and shall be glad when you have gone, but perhaps it may be because I am a wicked woman ; and I do not know what has come over me, that now I want to fly away from you, when I used to think that I had the best husband on all this earth." The potter sighed bitterly, but he kissed her cheeks, which felt as cold as ice, and then he said good-bye to his baby, and started on his way with the tears filling his eyes.

When the potter had gone the wife cried sorely, but still she was glad that she had not to see him, and for some time she lived with her baby happily enough. She kept the house, and mended and swept and cleaned as before, and thought little of the potter or where he had gone ; but by and by all her money began to be spent, and she knew that unless the potter returned she would soon be very poor, and the winter was coming on, and she feared cold and hunger for her little one. So she went into a garret where she kept her old weaving loom, and she brought it out, and she bought flax, and sat down to weave just as she used to, when she went round the country with her sister who spun the flax. And she found that she could still weave her cloths very skilfully, and she began to sell them to the passers by, and in this way she earned her bread.

The winter set in very cold and hard, and the potter's wife felt very sad. "But perhaps," she said, "it is thinking of the poor things who are starving around with no homes," for she never thought of her husband at all. And the flax began to be very dear, and she had difficulty in buying it. "Instead of doing all these cheap cloths," she said, "it would be better to get very fine flax, and do a very very fine cloth; it will be the finest cloth I have ever woven, and I will sell it to some very rich lady." So she bought the finest flax that money could bring her, and when she had woven a little bit of it, she sat and looked at it in her room, and she saw a tress of her own golden hair lying upon it, and she thought how beautiful it looked. Then she said—

" There is no one now who loves me or my hair, so I will weave it into a cloth with this very fine flax, and I must sell it for a very large sum of money, or else I shall have nothing left to go on with." But she couldn't think of any pattern in which the hair looked well with the fine linen flax, till at last she hit on one in which there was a cup with a heart on the top of it. The cup she made of the gold hair, and the heart also. She worked at it for many long days, and when she had finished it she looked at it, and was very much pleased, and said indeed it was the most beautiful cloth she had ever made; and now she must make haste and take it in to the town and sell it for a great deal of money, or she and her child would begin to do badly for food and fire.

The snow was lying heavily upon the ground, as the potter's wife stood by the window looking at her cloth, when there crawled up outside the window a poor gipsy woman leading a little boy by the hand. She had big black eyes and a brown face, but her cheeks were so thin that the colour scarcely showed in them, and the potter himself would have had much ado to recognize her as the gipsy girl who made the cup years before ; and her clothes all hung upon her in rags, and her little boy was crying bitterly with the cold. She knocked against the window with her poor thin hands. " Take me in," she cried, "and have pity on me, for I can go no further." Then the potter's wife opened the door, and the gipsy woman entered the room with her little boy by her side, and crouched by the fire.

"Where is the potter who lived here?" said the gipsy. " It is long years ago since I saw him, and now I have come back to pray that he would give me food, for I am starving,"

" No," said the wife, " I know not where he is, for he is my husband, and he has left me, and right glad of it am I ; but if you will stay here I will give you food and drink and attend to you, for, poor woman, you seem to me to be very ill ; so stay here and I will attend to you till you are well enough to go your way."

" There is only one way that I shall ever go," said the gipsy, and she looked into the fire with her big black eyes, "and that is the road which leads to the churchyard. But if he was your husband, why do you say that you are glad he is away ? Is he not kind to you ? "

"He was very kind to me," said the potter's wife, "he gave me everything I wanted, and money and to spare, but for all that I could not love him, and I am glad he has gone, and left me alone with my baby girl."

"You are a foolish woman," said the gipsy. "If you had a husband who loved you and worked for you well, you should have loved him and cherished him. My husband beat me, and was cruel to me, and stole all I had. And now that I am dying, he has deserted me to die as I may."

Then the potter's wife brought her food and bid her lie down, and dried her rags of clothes, and she wrapped the little boy in her own clothes, and gave him food and put him to sleep; and as she lay, the gipsy woman watched her with her great black eyes, and at last she said, "Have you a brown cup here, a little rough brown cup? did your husband give it to you?"

The potter's wife stared with astonishment. "How did you know I had a little rough brown cup?" she said. "There was such a one, and it stood upon the shelf, but I have given it away. I gave it to a poor gipsy man who begged it of me; he wanted it so badly that I couldn't refuse, and he made me drink his health in it ere he took it away."

Then the gipsy woman raised her head, and her eyes looked blacker and her cheeks blacker.

"And what was the gipsy man like?" she cried. "Had you drunk from the cup before? Can you remember?"

"I remember well," said the woman. "I drank from it on the day when I promised I would marry my husband, and I drank from it once again when I wished the gipsy God-speed, and soon after that, my husband left me, for I could not bear to have him near me."

Then the gipsy cried out aloud, and said something in a language which the woman did not understand, and beat her hands.

"I think it was my husband," she said. "Alack a day! to-morrow night I shall die, and who will take care of my little boy, and see that he does not starve? for his father would beat and ill-treat him if he found him." Then the potter's wife kneeled down beside the gipsy woman, and kissed her on the forehead.

"Be at peace," she said. "If it be that you must die, die with a quiet heart, for I will keep your little boy. What is enough for two is enough for three, and he shall call my little girl sister and me mother."

The gipsy said nothing, but she looked at the potter's wife for long, and then she said, "And my clothes are all in rags, and I have no garment in which you can wrap me for my grave."

Then the potter's wife began to cry. "Be at peace," she said, "for I have a fine cloth made of flax and my own hair, and in it you can lie clad like a princess."

Then again the gipsy woman cried out words that the potter's wife did not understand, and again she beat her breast and lamented. But as evening drew nigh she turned to the potter's wife, and told her all the truth about the charms in the cup, and wept for the evil she had done her, who was so good and kind.

The potter's wife sat by her all that day, and into the dark hours of the night, but when it was drawing nigh to twelve o'clock the gipsy woman sat up, and stretched out her arms. " The wheel," she cried, " bring me your husband's wheel, and give me a piece of clay, that while there is yet time I may throw my last cup, and you may drink from it before the dawn and undo the harm I have worked."

The potter's wife wondered much, but she feared to disobey her, and she went out into her husband's workshop, and she brought in his wheel and a piece of clay which stood there, and placed them beside the gipsy. The gipsy was so weak that she could scarcely sit up, but when she saw the wheel she staggered to her feet, and took the clay in her thin little brown hands, and moulded it as she had done years before ; and then she set it on the wheel, and set the wheel spinning, and formed it into a little brown bowl, and bent her head over it, and whispered into it.

" Now drink," she cried, "although the clay is still wet. Pour water into it and drink from my little bowl, and wish me God-speed as you did to my husband. And then dress me in white and gold like a princess, for I must start upon my journey. But keep my little boy always, and if my husband comes to search for me, give him my ring, but tell him that he shall never find me more."

The potter's wife poured some water into the little clay cup, and stooped her face and drank it, that the woman might be content, and when she had done so, the gipsy folded her hands and lay back and died. But when she had tasted the water out of the wet clay, the potter's wife thought of her husband, and she called his name, and cried to him to come and help her with the poor gipsy woman. And then she thought of how long it was since he had been with her, and she began to cry, and wept bitterly as she leant over the dead woman.

"Oh, where is he gone? why did I drive him from me?" she said. "Have I been mad? Truly the poor gipsy spoke rightly, that if a woman has a husband who loves her and works for her, she should cherish him with all her might. Alas, alas! and now my husband is out in the wide world, and I am alone here with no one to help me; until this poor woman told me, I never knew how wrong I was." Then she looked at the gipsy woman lying in all her rags, and she remembered her promise to her, and she took the fine linen cloth in which was woven the gold heart and the gilt cup, and she clothed her in it as if she were a princess, and the next day the poor woman was buried, and no one knew from whence she came nor to whom she belonged.

Then the potter's wife sat down, and grieved bitterly, for she didn't know what it would be best to do to find her husband again, and tell him that she loved him as at first. At first she thought she would go out and seek for him in the wide, wide world, but then she remembered how he bid her wait where she was till he came back, and she knew she ought to do what he had told her; but as now she had three to keep instead of two, she feared they would be very poor, and as she had buried the gipsy in the fine gold and white cloth woven with her hair, she had not got it to sell, and she had not any money left wherewith to buy more fine thread to weave. The gipsy's little boy was a pretty boy, with dark eyes like his mother's, and when she looked at him she said they would all three starve together, but she would keep him, as she had promised his mother, rather than turn him out into the cold streets. So she washed him, and mended his rags as best she might, and then she began to seek everywhere for something she might weave to sell, and keep them from starving. She wandered round the garden, and in and out of the house, and the gipsy boy, who was a clever, bright lad, went with her.

" What are you searching for ? " he asked.

" I am searching for thread, that I may weave into some kind of cloth and sell," she said. " Otherwise we shall surely starve, for I have no money left to buy it with, and nothing more left to sell."

" I will go and get you something to weave," said the boy, and he ran out into the road, and looked up and down it to see what would come past. Presently there came up a big cart laden with straw, and on the top of the cart lay one man, while another drove. The horses went slowly, and the gipsy boy followed them, and began to beg.

" Run off, little chap," cried the man at the top, " I have no money to give to beggars."

" But I don't ask you for money," cried the boy, " but of your charity give me a handful of straw."

" And what do you want with a handful of straw ? " asked the carter, as the boy still went on begging.

" Why, see ! " cried the lad, " I am all in rags, but if my mother had a handful of straw she can weave me a coat, and I shall be quite warm," at which the men both laughed, and declared that the idea of a coat of straw was very funny, but the driver said, " Well, give some to the little chap. I expect he comes from a lot of lying gipsies further on, and they want it for their animals, still it won't do any harm to give him a few wisps," and so they flung down a bundle, and the boy picked it up, and ran back with it to the potter's wife.

" See what I have brought you," he cried. " Now make that into a mat, and I will take it out and sell it, and bring you back the money."

The potter's wife was amazed by his cleverness, but she knew that the gipsies had to live by their wits, and that teaches them to be sharp, so she sat down, and tried to weave the straw into a mat, as the gipsy boy had said.

At first she found it very hard to use, for it was coarse and brittle, and she thought she could make nothing of it. The lad sat beside her, and cut it into even lengths for her, and chose out the good pieces, and at last betwixt them it was done, and it looked quite a smart little mat, and the boy took it on his back and ran away with it to the village.

"A mat, a mat," he cried, "who wants to buy a good straw mat to wipe their feet on when they are dirty, or for the cat to sit on by the fire, or to put over the fowl-house and keep it warm?"

At first all the people he met laughed at him, and said nobody wished to buy a mat at all. Then he turned into the ale-house. There were some men smoking and keeping themselves warm by the fire, and when the host saw him, and the mat over his shoulder, he said it was quite a well-made thing, and he would have it to lay down by his doorway for in-comers to tread on; and then one and another looked at it, and the boy told them where it came from, and said he could bring them plenty more straw mats and carpets, all as good or better, and so well worked that they would last almost for ever; and presently one and another began to say that they would buy them, and when he had taken his money, the gipsy boy ran home well content.

So the potter's wife sat all day weaving straw mats, and presently she got to do them so well, that from far and near the people sent to buy them of her. Then after a time she put patterns into them, made with red, and black, and white straws, but do what she could, the patterns always came out in the shape of a cup, and still she wept and grieved all day long. Then the gipsy lad said to her—

"What are you crying for now? You have plenty to eat and drink. Tell me why you are crying, and I will help you if I can, because you took my mother into your house to die, and buried her in your fine cloth like a princess."

"I cry because my husband has gone a long way off," said the potter's wife, "and he doesn't know that I love him, and he will never come back to me, for when he went away I hated him."

"He will never know it if you don't try to tell him," said the gipsy boy. "You should tell it to every one you meet, to all the birds of the air, and the wild animals too. That is what my mother told me to do, if I wanted to send news abroad. You should say it even to the winds, and write it in the sand, and on the earth, and on the leaves of the trees in case they blow about, for she said all things could pass on a secret, though none can keep one. And why don't you weave it into your mats too? For the people who buy them take them far and near, and maybe he will see one, and know that you want him to come home again."

Then the potter's wife tried to weave her secret into her mats, and beside the pattern of the cup she wove a little verse—

> " From the gipsy's cup I drank for love,
> From the gipsy's cup I drank for hate,
> But when she gave me a cup again
> My love had gone and I drank too late."

" Now," cried the gipsy boy, "your husband may see it, and perhaps he will come home, and all will be well with us."

But still the potter journeyed far into the world, and wherever he went he asked if any gipsy had been near there ; and if there happened to be a gipsy camp in the neighbourhood, he went to it at once, and asked for a gipsy woman with red beads and gold chains in her hair, or for a gipsy man who carried a brown cup with him. But though he saw hundreds of gipsies, yet he never again saw the girl who had thrown the cup, and none of the men knew anything about the man, nor could tell him anything about the little brown bowl. Then he went to the shops in the big towns where jars and bowls

are sold, and asked for a cup that had a spell
in it, for he thought if they sold such a one, they
might know how to help him to undo the work
of the gipsy's bowl, but everywhere the people
only laughed at him.

So he went through strange countries, seeing
strange things, but none of them gave him any
pleasure, since he was always thinking of his wife
at home. Then he returned to his native land,
and pondered whether he should go back to his
own cottage, but his heart failed him, and he
kept far from the little village where it stood.

" It would be little use to go home," he said,
"for if my wife is not glad to see me, it is no
home to me ; and she will not be glad to see
me till I can find the gipsy and know how the
charm can be broken."

One night he went into a booth where there
were a number of men drinking, and amongst
them there was one who looked like a gipsy, a
dark, savage-looking fellow who was talking loud,
and boasting much of all he had done. The
potter sat and listened to their talk, and presently
they began quarrelling, and talking about who
was the most beautiful woman in the world. The

gipsy cried out that he knew the most beautiful, and that she had given him a parting gift and wished him God-speed, and now he was going back to her, for he knew now the way to make her love him, and he meant to wed her and have her for his wife.

Upon this the others laughed and jeered, and said, was it likely that such a beautiful woman would care for such a rough, ill-favoured fellow as he, and declared they didn't think much of her beauty if she was willing to marry him and to be his wife.

Then another man standing near said that he knew where lived the most beautiful woman on the face of the earth, though he did not believe that she would ever be wife of his, still all the same it would be hard to beat her for loveliness ; and she was a clever worker too, for she it was who worked the mats that lay under his feet in the cart he drove.   Upon this they all began to wrangle, and their words grew high.

" And if the beautiful woman loved you so," cried one man to the gipsy, " how could you come away and leave her ? "

The gipsy laughed. " She didn't love me

then," he said, "but she will now, for I am taking her a charm which will make her love me more than any one on earth. She has only to drink out of the cup I carry here, and she will be mine for life."

Upon this they all laughed, and derided him still more.

"Then let every one believe that what I say is true," cried the gipsy, and from his bosom he took out a small brown bowl and waved it in the air, "and here is the cup to prove it." And the potter's heart almost stood still, for he recognized the cup which the gipsy girl had made for him years before.

The other man laughed scornfully. "That proves nothing," he said. "I might take the mat out from the cart and ask it to say if I spoke the truth ; but mats and cups have no tongues to speak with, though my mat can say more than your cup, for there is a rhyme on it with a pattern of a cup ; moreover, the rhyme is about a gipsy too."

"Let us see it," cried they all.

Then the man went out to his cart and fetched in a white and brown straw mat, covered with

a pattern made of cups, and he read the rhyme
which was written upon it—

> "From the gipsy's cup I drank for love,
> From the gipsy's cup I drank for hate,
> And when she gave me that cup again
> My love was gone and I drank too late."

On hearing this the potter jumped up, and
dashed into their midst, and seized the cup.

"The gipsy speaks truth," he cried, "when
he says she is the most beautiful woman in the
world, but he speaks false when he says that she
will ever love him ; for he has stolen that cup,
and I shall take it from him, and if he tries to
stop me, why then I will fight him, and let every
one see who is the better fellow of the two."

But when the gipsy had seen the rhyme upon
the mat, he stood and stared as if he were made
of stone, and said no word to the potter, and
indeed scarcely seemed to notice that he had
taken away the cup from him. Then the potter
turned to the man who owned the mat and said,
"If you will sell me your mat I will pay you
handsomely for it, and I beg you to tell me who
made it, and where you got it, for I would like
to buy some more like it."

The traveller was much astonished, but he told the potter that it was made by a woman who lived in a village a little way off, and she sat by her doorway and wove mats, with a gipsy boy to help her ; and she was the loveliest woman he had ever seen on earth, with eyes just like blue cornflowers and hair like golden corn. Then the potter took his bowl and the mat and started to go home, but the gipsy slunk out of the room and went into the night, and nobody noticed him.

Meantime the potter's wife continued to grieve and lament, for in spite of her taking the gipsy boy's advice, and telling all things that she loved her husband and wished him back, he did not come back to her ; and though she wove her rhyme into every mat that she made, she despaired of the potter's ever seeing one. The only thing which seemed to console her, was the little brown clay cup that the gipsy woman had thrown for her, before she died. As it had never been baked in the oven, the clay was dry and hard and cracked, and it was a sorry thing to look at, but still the potter's wife kept it beside her, and would drink out of nothing else, and from time to time she kissed it, and laid her cheek against it.

The gipsy boy said to her—

"If I were you I should watch for my husband all day. I would weave my mats in the doorway, and look up the road both ways, from morn till night, otherwise your husband will come back and go past the cottage and you will never know." So she took her loom and sat by the roadway, and watched, and looked over the hill and to right and left for whoever might come. And often the gipsy boy would watch too, and look from the other side of the cottage while the potter's wife sat in the front. One day the gipsy boy ran round to her and said, "There is some one coming up the road who will come here, but it is not your husband. It is my father, and he will want to take me away, and he will beat me as he did my mother. And if he gets hold of the cup that my mother made for you, he knows all her charms, and he can undo what she did, and perhaps can throw some evil spell on us all, so that your husband will never return again. So the best thing will be for you to give me the cup and let me hide myself with it, and then you must tell him that you do not know where I am, and if he asks, tell him that the cup is gone; and when he is gone I will come back again, but promise that you will not give me up to him."

So the potter's wife promised that she would never give up the little boy, and she bid him take the cup and run quickly and hide himself, and then she took her little girl by the hand and sat and waited for the gipsy man to come, though she trembled with fear, and wished him far away.

Presently the gipsy man came up to the front of the cottage where the potter's wife sat, and bid her good-day.

"I was here before," he said. "And you gave me something to eat and drink. Is your husband come back, for he was away then?"

"My husband is away still," she said. "But soon I hope he will be here."

Then the gipsy took up one of her mats which lay on the ground beside her, and looked at it.

"You are clever with your loom," he said; "but what do you mean by the little verse you put on all these mats?"

"It is a little verse which can but be rightly read by one person," she answered; "and if he sees it, it will not matter whether others understand it or no."

"And have you been here all alone since I came by?" asked the gipsy; "have no other gipsies been past? for I want to join some of my own people, and perhaps you can tell me which way they are gone."

"One came not so long ago," answered the potter's wife, "but she was so tired with tramping far that she could go no further. So she has stayed, and rests in the churchyard. She was a gipsy woman with red beads and coins in her hair. And I kept her and let her die in peace, and wrapped her in a cloth of white and gold."

"And did she do nothing while she rested here?" asked the gipsy man. "Did she make you no present to pay you for your trouble?"

"She made me a present which paid me for my trouble well," said the woman, "though it was only a little cup of clay that was grey and wet. And she gave me this ring, and bid me give it to her husband if he came by here, and tell him that it was useless for him to seek her further."

The gipsy man looked at the ring she held out to him, and he turned pale, and knit his brows.

"And where is that cup?" he asked; "and

where is her little boy ? For I will take him with me into the world."

" I don't know where he is gone," said the potter's wife ; "as for the cup, he took it with him when he went."

Meantime the gipsy boy had hidden in a hay-stack quite close to the cottage, from where he could see the roadways all round, and he looked to right and left for who should pass, for he was still half afraid that his father might come and search for him, and take him away by force. As he lay and watched he saw a man coming over the hill, who looked spent and tired, as if he had walked far. He seemed to know the path well, and he came straight to the cottage, but he did not come in, but waited near as if he wanted to see who was there. Then the gipsy boy said to himself—

" Perhaps this is the potter himself, whom she has been looking for all this time." So he slid down and ran to the man and began to pretend to beg.

The man looked at him and said—

" You are a gipsy's child. Where do you come from ? Are you living under a hedge, or do you come from a gipsy's camp near ? "

"It is true I am a gipsy's child," answered the boy, "but I am living under no hedge, but in that little cottage, for the woman who lives there keeps me for love of my mother, who helped her when she was in trouble."

"And what did your mother do for the woman?" asked the man, who was no other than the potter. "It must have been a great service, that she should be willing to take you and keep you."

"She saved her from an evil charm that had been cast upon her," answered the boy, "and taught her to love her husband again, and she waits his return now and longs for him to come. Therefore she promised to keep me with her, but now I dare not go into the cottage, because my father, who is a gipsy, is there, and I am afraid lest he may take me away with him."

When the potter heard that the gipsy man was there he would have run straight into the cottage, but the boy implored him to listen first and hear what he was saying. So they crept round to the side of the cottage, and they heard the gipsy man growing angry, and threatening the potter's wife, that if she did not tell him where

his boy had gone he would seize her by the hair
and wring her throat, in spite of her being so fair
a woman. At this the potter waited no longer,
but burst into the cottage, and seized the
gipsy and hurled him out of the house with all
his might ; but he and his wife never looked to
see if he was hurt or no, for they looked at
nothing but each other and the little child that
the potter's wife held by the hand. And the gipsy
man went away, and they never heard of him
again.

Then the potter's wife showed her husband the
gipsy boy, and told him of her promise to his
mother, and of all he had done for her, and
begged him that he would let her keep him with
them. And the potter promised that she should,
and said that when he grew up to be a man he
would teach him his trade, and make him a potter
like himself. So they all lived happily together,
and the gipsy boy learned to make cups and
bowls, and was very clever at doing them, but
they were cups and bowls that carried no charms
with them, and so could do no one any harm that
drank from them.

NCE there lived an old gentleman who was a very rich
old gentleman, and able
to buy nearly everything
he wanted. He had earned
all his wealth for himself
by trading in a big city,
and now he had grown so
fond of money that he
loved it better than anything else in the world, and
thought of nothing except how he could save it
up and make more. But he never seemed to
have time to enjoy himself with all that he had
earned, and he was very angry if he was asked to
give money to others. He lived in a handsome
house all alone, and he had a very good cook
who cooked him a sumptuous dinner every day,

128

but he rarely asked any one to share it with him, though he loved eating and drinking, and always had the best of wine and food. His cook and his other servants knew that he was greedy and hard, and cared for nobody, and though they served him well because he paid them, they none of them loved him.

It was one Christmas, and the snow lay thick upon the ground, and the wind howled so fiercely that the old gentleman was very glad he was not obliged to go out into the street, but could sit in his comfortable arm-chair by the fire and keep warm.

" It really is terrible weather," he said to himself, "terrible weather;" and he went to the window and looked out into the street, where all the pavements were inches deep in snow. " I am very glad that I need not go out at all, but can sit here and keep warm for to-day, that is the great thing, and I shall have some ado to keep out the cold even here with the fire."

He was leaving the window, when there came up in the street outside an old man, whose clothes hung in rags about him, and who looked half frozen. He was about the same age as the old gentleman inside the window, and the same height, and had grey, curly hair, like his, and if they had been dressed alike any one would have taken them for two brothers.

"Oh, really," said the old gentleman irritably, "this is most annoying. The parish ought to take up these sort of people, and prevent their wandering about the streets and molesting honest folk," for the poor old man had taken off his hat, and began to beg.

"It is Christmas Day," he said, and though he did not speak very loud, the old gentleman could hear every word he said quite plainly through the window. "It is Christmas Day, and you will have your dinner here in your warm room. Of your charity give me a silver shilling that I may go into an eating-shop, and have a dinner too."

"A silver shilling!" cried the old gentleman, "I never heard of such a thing! Monstrous! Go away, I never give to beggars, and you must have done something very wicked to become so poor."

But still the old man stood there, though the snow was falling on his shoulders, and on his bare head. "Then give me a copper," he said; "just one penny, that to-day I may not starve."

"Certainly not," cried the old gentleman ; " I tell you I never give to beggars at all." But the old man did not move.

"Then," he said, "give me some of the broken victuals from your table, that I may creep into a doorway and eat a Christmas dinner there."

"I will give you nothing," cried the old gentleman, stamping his foot. "Go away. Go away at once, or I shall send for the policeman to take you away."

The old beggar-man put on his hat and turned quietly away, but what the old gentleman thought was very odd was, that instead of seeming distressed he was laughing merrily, and then he looked back at the window, and called out some words, but they were in a foreign tongue, and the old gentleman could not understand them. So he returned to his comfortable arm-chair by the fire, still murmuring angrily that beggars ought not to be allowed to be in the streets.

Next morning the snow fell more thickly than ever, and the streets were almost impassable, but it did not trouble the old gentleman, for he knew he need not go out and get wet or cold. But in the morning when he came down to breakfast, to his great surprise there was a cat on the hearthrug in front of the fire, looking into it, and blinking lazily. Now the old gentleman had never had any animal in his house before, and he at once went to it and said "Shoo-shoo!" and tried to turn it out. But the cat did not move, and when the old gentleman looked at it nearer, he could not help admiring it very much. It was a very large cat, grey and black, and had extremely long soft hair, and a thick soft ruff round its neck. Moreover, it looked very well fed and cared for, and as if it had always lived in comfortable places. Somehow it seemed to the old gentleman to suit the room and the rug and the fire, and to make the whole place look more prosperous and cosy even than it had done before.

"A fine creature! a very handsome cat!" he said to himself; "I should really think that a reward would be offered for such an animal, as it has evidently been well looked after and fed, so it would be a pity to turn it away in a hurry."

One thing struck him as very funny about the cat, and that was that though the ground was deep in snow and slush outside, the cat was quite dry, and its fur looked as if it had just been combed and brushed. The old gentleman called to his cook and asked if she knew how the cat had come in, but she declared she had not seen it before, and said she believed it must have come down the chimney as all the doors and windows had been shut and bolted. However, there it was, and when his own breakfast was finished the old gentleman gave it a large saucer of milk, which it lapped up not greedily or in a hurry, but as if it were quite used to good food and had had plenty of it always.

"It really is a very handsome animal, and most uncommon," said the old gentleman, " I shall keep it awhile and look out for the reward;" but though he looked at all the notices in the street and in the newspapers, the old gentleman could see no notice about a reward being offered for a grey and black cat, so it stayed on with him from day to day.

Every day the cat seemed to his master to grow handsomer and handsomer. The old gentleman never loved anything but himself, but he began to take a sort of interest in the strange cat, and to wonder what sort it was—if it was a Persian or a Siamese, or some curious new sort of which he had never heard. He liked the sound of its lazy contented purring after its food, which seemed to speak of nothing but comfort and affluence. So the cat remained on till nearly a year had passed away.

It was not very long before Christmas that an acquaintance of the old gentleman's came to his rooms on business. He knew a great deal about all sorts of animals and loved them for their own sakes, but of course he had never talked to the old gentleman about them, because he knew he did not love anything. But when he saw the grey cat, he said at once—

"Do you know that this is a very valuable creature, and I should think would be worth a great deal?"

At these words the old gentleman's heart beat high. Here, he thought, would be a piece of great luck if a stray cat could make him richer than he was before.

" Why, who would want to buy it?" he said. "I don't know anybody who would be so foolish as to give any money for a cat which is of no use in life except to catch mice, when you can so easily get one for nothing."

"Ah, but many people are very fond of cats, and would give much for rare sorts like this. If you want to sell it, the right thing would be to send it to the Cat Show, and there you would most likely take a prize for it, and then some one would be sure to buy it, and, it may be, would give a great deal. I don't know what kind it is, or where it comes from, for I have never seen one the least like it, but for that reason it is very sure to be valuable."

Upon this the old gentleman almost laughed with joy.

"Where is the Cat Show?" he asked; "and when is it to be held?"

"There will be a Cat Show in this city quite soon," said his acquaintance; "and it will be a particularly good one, for the new Princess is quite crazy about cats, and she is coming to it, and it is said that she doesn't mind what she gives for a cat if she sees one she likes."

So then he told the old gentleman how he should send his name and the cat's name to the people who managed the show, and where it was to be held, and went away, leaving the old gentleman well pleased, but to himself he laughed and

said, " I don't think that old man thinks of anything on earth but making money.   How pleased
he was at the idea of selling that beautiful cat if
he could get something for it ! "

When he had gone, the grey puss came and
rubbed itself about his master's legs, and looked
up in his face as though it had understood the
conversation, and did not like the idea of being
sent to the show.   But the old gentleman was
delighted, and sat by the fire and mused on what
he was likely to get for the cat, and wondered if
it would not take a prize.

" I shall be sorry to have to send it away," he
said ; " still, if I could get a good round sum of
money it would be a real sin not to take it, so you
will have to go, puss ; and it really was extraordinary good luck for me that you ever came
here."

The days passed, and Christmas Day came, and
again the snow fell, and the ground was white.
The wind whistled and blew, and on Christmas
morning the old gentleman stood and looked out
of the window at the falling snow and rain, and
the grey cat stood beside him, and rubbed itself
against his hand.   He rather liked stroking it, it

was so soft and comfortable, and when he touched the long hair he always thought of how much money he should get for it.

This morning he saw no old beggar-man outside the window, and he said to himself: "I really think they manage better with the beggars than they used to, and are clearing them from the town."

But just as he was leaving the window he heard something scratching outside, and there crawled on to the window-sill another cat. It was a very different creature to the grey cat on the rug. It was a poor, thin, wretched-looking animal, with ribs sticking through its fur, and it mewed in the most pathetic manner, and beat itself against the pane. When it saw it, the handsome grey puss was very much excited, and ran to and fro, and purred loudly.

"Oh you disgraceful-looking beast!" said the old gentleman angrily; "go away, this is not the place for an animal like you. There is nothing here for stray cats. And you look as if you had not eaten anything for months. How different to my puss here!" and he tapped against the window to drive it away. But still it would not go, and the old gentleman felt very indignant, for the sound of its mewing was terrible. So he opened the window, and though he did not like to touch the miserable animal, he took it up and hurled it away into the snow, and it trotted away, and in the deep snow he could not see the way it went.

But that evening, after he had had his Christmas dinner, as he sat by the fire with the grey puss on the hearthrug beside him, he heard again the noise outside the window, and then he heard the stray cat crying and mewing to be let in, and again the grey and black cat became very much excited, and dashed about the room, and jumped at the window as if it wanted to open it.

" I shall really be quite glad when I have sold you at the Cat Show," said the old gentleman, " if I am going to have all sorts of stray cats worrying here," and for the second time he opened the window, and seized the trembling, half-starved creature, and this time he threw it with all his might as hard as he could throw. " And now there is an end of you, I hope," he said as he heard it fall with a dull thud, and settled himself again in his arm-chair, and the grey puss returned to the hearthrug, but it did not purr or rub itself against its master.

Next morning when he came down to breakfast, the old gentleman poured out a saucer of milk for his cat as usual. " You must be well fed if you are going to be shown at the show," he said, " and I must not mind a little extra expense to make you look well. It will all be paid back, so this morning you shall have some fish as well as your milk." Then he put the saucer of milk down by the cat, but it never touched it, but sat and looked at the fire with its tail curled round it.

" Oh, well, if you have had so much already that you don't want it, you can take it when you do," so he went away to his work and left the saucer of milk by the fire. But when he came back in the evening there was the saucer of milk and the piece of fish, and the grey cat had not touched them. " This is rather odd," said the old gentleman ; "however, I suppose cook has been feeding you."

Next morning it was just the same. When he poured out the milk the cat wouldn't lap it, but sat and looked at the fire. The old gentleman felt a little anxious, for he fancied that the animal's

fur did not look so bright as usual, and when in
the evening and the next day and the next, it
would not lap its milk, or even smell the nice
pieces of fish he gave it, he was really uncomfortable. "The creature is getting ill," he said, "and
this is most provoking. "What will be the use
of my having kept it for a year, if now I cannot show it?" He scolded his cook for having given it unwholesome food, but the cook
swore it had had nothing. Anyhow it was
growing terribly thin, and all day long it sat in
front of the fire with its tail hanging down,
not curled up neatly round it, and its coat
looked dull and began to come out in big tufts
of hair.

"Now really I shall have to do something,"
said the old gentleman, "it is enough to make any
one angry! No one would believe that this could
be a prize cat. It looks almost as wretched as
that stray beast that came to the window on
Christmas Day." So he went to a cat and dog
doctor, who lived near, and asked him to come
in and see a very beautiful cat which had
nothing the matter with it, but which refused to
eat its food. The cat's doctor came and looked

at the cat, and then looked very grave, and shook his head, and looked at it again.

" I don't know what sort of cat it is," he said, " for I never saw any other like it, but it is a very handsome beast, and must be very valuable. Well, I will leave you some physic for it, and I hope you may be able to pull it round, but with these foreign cats you never know what ails them, and they are hard to cure."

Now the day was close at hand when the cat should have been sent to the show, and the old gentleman was getting more and more uneasy, for the grey cat lay upon the rug all day and never moved, and its ribs could almost be seen through its side, so thin had it grown. And oddly enough the old gentleman, who had never cared for any one or anything in his life except himself, began to feel very unhappy, not only because of not getting the money, but because he did not like to think of losing the cat itself. He sent for his friend who had first told him about the Cat Show, and asked his advice, but his friend could not tell him what to do with it.

" Well, well," he said, " this is a bad business, for I have told every one that you are going to exhibit a most extraordinarily beautiful cat, and now this poor creature is really fit for nothing but the knacker's yard. I think, maybe, some naturalist would give you a good price for its skin, as it is so very uncommon, and if I were you I should kill it at once, for if it dies a natural death its skin won't be worth a brass farthing." At these words the grey cat lifted its head, and looked straight into the old gentleman's face, as if it could understand, and for the first time for many a long year, the old gentleman felt a feeling of pity in his heart, and was angry with his friend for his suggestion.

" I won't have it killed," he cried ; " why, I declare, though it does seem absurd, I have lived with this creature for a year, and I feel as if it were my friend, and if it would only get well and sit up on the hearthrug, I shouldn't mind about the money one bit ! "

At this his friend was greatly astonished, and went away wondering, while the old gentleman sat by the fire and watched the cat lying panting on the rug.

" Poor pussy, poor old pussy ! " he said, " it is a pity that you can't speak and tell me what you

want. I am sure I would give it to you." Just
as he spoke there came a noise outside, and he
heard a mewing, and looking through the window
he saw the same thin ugly brown cat that had
come there last Christmas, and it looked as thin
and wretched as ever. When she heard the sound
the grey cat stood up on her tottering feet and
tried to walk to the window This time the old
gentleman did not drive it away, but looked at it,
and almost felt sorry for it ; it looked almost as
thin and ill as his own grey puss.

" You are an ugly brute," he said, " and I don't
want you always hanging about ; still, maybe you
would be none the worse for a little milk now, and
it might make you look better." So he opened
the window a little, and then he shut it and then
he opened it again, and this time the brown cat
crawled into the room, and went straight to the
hearthrug to the grey puss. There was a big
saucer of milk on the hearthrug, and the brown
cat began to lap it at once, and the old gentleman
never stopped it.

He thought as he watched it, that it grew fatter
under his eyes as it drank, and when the saucer
was empty he took a jug and gave it some more.

"I really am an old fool," he said ; "that is a whole pennorth of milk." No sooner had he poured out the fresh milk than the grey cat raised itself, and sitting down by the saucer began to lap it as well, as if it were quite well. The old gentleman stared with surprise. "Well, this is the queerest thing," he said. So he took some fish and gave it to the strange cat, and then, when

he offered some to his own puss, it ate it as if there was nothing the matter. "This is most remarkable," said the old gentleman ; "perhaps it was the company of a creature of its own sort that my cat needed, after all." And the grey cat purred and began to rub itself against his legs.

So for the next few days the two cats lay together on the hearthrug, and though it was too late to send the grey cat to the show, the old

gentleman never thought about it, so pleased was
he that it had got well again.

But seven nights after the stray cat had come
in from outside, as the old gentleman lay asleep
in bed at night, he felt something rub itself against
his face, and heard his cat purring softly, as though

it wanted to say " good-bye." " Be quiet, puss,
and lie still till the morning," he said. But when
he came down to have his breakfast in the morning, there sat the brown tabby, looking fat and
comfortable by the fire, but the grey cat was not
there, and though they looked for it everywhere,

L

no one could find it, though all the windows and doors had been shut, so they could not think how it could have got away. The old gentleman was very unhappy about it, but he looked at the strange cat on his hearth and said, "it would be unkind now to send this poor thing away, so it may as well stay here."

When she heard him speaking of its being un-kind, his old cook burst out laughing. "Perhaps," she said, " 'twas a fairy cat, as it could get away through bolts and locks, and nothing but a fairy could have taught my master to think of a thing being unkind or not. I only hope that now he'll think of some one in this world besides himself and his money." And sure enough from that time the old gentleman began to forget about his money, and to care for the people about him, and it was all the doing of the strange cat who had come from no one knew where, and gone away to no one knew where.

DUMB OTHMAR

NCE upon a time there was a village on the top of a mountain, where during the winter months the villagers saw no one but each other, for the mountain was so steep and the path so narrow that, when it was blocked with ice, it was dangerous to ascend: so during the winter months the people lived by themselves, and cheered themselves as they might in the long dreary evenings, with games and dancing and singing and playing on pipes, for they were cheerful folk, joyous and light - hearted. The

147

sweetest singer in the village was a lad named Othmar; his voice was as sweet as a nightingale's before the dawn, and also he was the handsomest young fellow in all the country round. Strangers turned to look after him as he went by; he was tall and straight, and had curly brown hair, and big brown eyes, and lips that always smiled. He lived with his old mother, who was a widow, and he worked for them both in the fields and on the farms. When he was a boy he learned the notes of all the birds, and could imitate them so exactly that they would fly down to him and settle on his shoulders. When the farmers had sown their fields, and the birds would have come to pick up the grain, they sent for Othmar, and he sang and whistled till they all left the field and flew after him. So often he was called the bird-boy.

One evening before the winter had set in, or the roads were blocked with ice, there came along the high road into the village, a dwarf in a yellow cap leading a donkey, on whose back were fastened numberless musical instruments. Fiddles of all sorts, and viols, horns, trumpets, and pipes, and a big drum, and a small one with triangles and cymbals. In the middle of the village the little man stopped and looked about him. "Who would like to hear my music?" he cried, and then as the villagers came crowding around him, he bade them all sit down while he unpacked his mule, but he forbade any of them to help him, or to touch one of the instruments. "For mine is no common music," he quoth; "all these I have made myself, and in each is a machine which makes it go on playing by itself, if once I start it. See here!" and he took up a long pipe and began to blow, and there came forth the sweetest notes that had ever been heard from any pipe. The little man paused for a minute, with the pipe in his hand, and then laid it down on the ground, when, wonderful to relate, it went on playing of itself.

All the villagers stared with surprise, and some called out that it was magic, and crossed themselves, but the little man took up another pipe, and set that going too, and then the horns and the trumpets, and the drums and the cymbals, and then he took a fiddle and drew the bow across it, and how it played! It made the people weep and laugh. Othmar lay on the ground listening, and it seemed to him as if the sound were made of silver, and when the musician had started them, and all the other fiddles were playing together, he felt as if he should go mad for joy to hear anything so lovely.

Just behind where Othmar lay sat a young girl, named Hulda. She was an orphan, and dwelt alone with an old woman, who gave her food and lodging for sweeping out her room, and cleaning and cooking. Also Hulda made money for her by going out to work for the other women in the village. She was neither pretty nor clever, but she was a good girl, and if any of the villagers were ill or in trouble, it was for Hulda they would send at once, because they knew she would spare no pains to help them, and would think nothing too much trouble. She had played with Othmar ever since they were babies, and loved him dearly. She was the only one who listened to the music who did not think it beautiful. She shuddered as she heard it, and she sat and watched Othmar and saw that there were tears in his eyes, and she grieved that she did not love it as he did.

When at last the instruments stopped and

the listeners began to feel for money for the musician, he laughed and said, " You need not give me money, for I am very rich, and don't need it. In return for my playing, I only ask for one recompense. Let any of your young folks who sing, sing me a song, for I too love hearing music that is not my own." On this the villagers began to look round for all who could sing, and they chose out some three or four, and begged them to sing their very best to the wonderful musician. Among them was Othmar, but they all bid him wait to the last, as his would be the best. Whilst the others were singing, the little man did not seem to heed them much, though they tried hard to sing well, and chose their prettiest songs, but their voices sounded very rough and poor after the playing.

But when Othmar began he stopped twanging the fiddle-strings and watched him. Othmar's voice rang out clear and sweet, and all the village folk felt proud of his singing, even after hearing the wonderful instruments. When he ceased the little man rose, and said—

" You have a sweet voice, my boy, be sure that you always use it well ; and now I must be going my way, but as I am a stranger here, perhaps you would not mind setting me on my road, and showing me the best way over the hill."

Othmar sprang up, delighted to go with him, but Hulda, who watched from behind, came up to him and whispered—

"Oh, Othmar, don't let him take you far—come back soon."

"How silly you are, Hulda!" said Othmar, almost angrily. "Of course I shall come back, but I shall go with him as far as he wants, and then, perhaps, he will let me hear him play again."

Othmar and the little dwarf started with the mule laden with instruments, and Othmar led the way down the best road. The dwarf did not speak at all, and so they went on in silence till they had got on to the top of a high hill where they could see the country all round for miles, and the moon was beginning to rise. Here the musician stopped his mule, and stood for a while looking all round. Then he turned, and said to Othmar—"I know now where I am, and here will I stay for to-night, but first before you leave me, would you not like to hear my fiddles and horns again?"

"That I would," cried Othmar, and he sat himself down on the ground delighted, while the little man unloaded the mule.

"And now," he said to Othmar with a twisted smile, "you shall hear them play as no one has ever heard them. Yes, and you shall see them too;" then he laid them in rows—the fiddles first, and the viols, and then the horns and trumpets, and last the drums and cymbals and triangles, and clapped his hands, giving a long, shrill whistle. As he whistled, the instruments rose from the ground, and they began to swell, and their shapes to change till no longer did they look like musical instruments, but like human beings, only each had in a strange way kept the shape it had formerly. The flutes and pipes were tall and thin, and they and the violins had changed into beautiful girls with slender throats, and the trumpets were all men and boys of different sizes, but the drum was the strangest of all, for it was a fat man with very short legs. The moon had risen and Othmar could see them all quite clearly, and though he trembled with fear and his heart beat high, yet still he watched. They stood silent together for a space in a weird crowd,

and then the dwarf waved his arms and called,
"Ay! are you all there, my children?—yes, one, two
three four five, six seven eight, nine ten eleven
twelve, thirteen—that is right.   Come practice,
practice, practice, and then you shall have a game,
and see who Othmar loves best, and who he will
kiss first."

Then they all began to sing together, but each
voice was like the sound of its own instrument,
only it said words through its tones, and in
Othmar's ears their music sounded as never music
had sounded before.   The voices of the violin
girls were so sweet that he felt as if he must weep
to hear them, while the sound of the pipes and
trumpets filled him with longing to go into the
world and fight and win battles.   He sat on the
ground and listened to them like one in a trance,
and he felt as if he never wished to rise or go
away again.   The dwarf sat on a hillock near, and
did not seem to heed them much.   When Othmar
took his eyes from the dancers for a minute, he
found that the place was quite full of all the
animals who are never seen by day, but who fly
out by night.   There were crowds of bats and
owls, and odd moths, all poised in the air, and

seeming to watch the musicians and listen to their singing. Then when he looked on the ground, he saw that strange wood-snakes and toads had come out boldly, and with their heads turned towards the dancers remained motionless and watched them, whilst near him green and brown lizards lay still as stone, with heads on one side, all staring through the dusky night at the singers. Othmar thought he only had watched them for a few minutes, when suddenly the dwarf cried out—" The dawn, the dawn, my children ; see, there is red in the sky. Come, be quick, see who will win Othmar's gift before we go on our way." When he was silent all the singing girls approached Othmar, but before the others came one who looked slighter and younger, and whose voice though as sweet was weaker.

" See, Othmar," she cried, " before we go on and leave you, let us try to sing one song together. Sing you as I do." And Othmar sang with her as she sang, in a clear voice like a bird's—

> " Ere the sun shines in the sky,
>   We will sing together, my love and I ;
>   But none shall hear him sing again,
>   'Neath moon or sun, in shine or rain."

And then ere the last notes had left Othmar's mouth, she bent forward, and clasped him in her slender arms, and kissed him on the lips while still they were open to sing.

"Good-bye, Othmar," cried she, "and that will be your last note for many a long year, for surely you will have no need to sing after I am gone," and at that all the strange folk standing near gave a laugh that was more a chord of music than a laugh. And when her lips touched Othmar's he quivered all over as a fiddle-string does when the bow is drawn across it; and he gave a cry which was like the sweet sound of a bell.

"Mine, mine!" cried the girl, as he fell back from her frightened. "Now my voice will be the sweetest and best of all, for I have got Othmar's too. No one will hear Othmar now,—Othmar who sang like the birds. And never will he call the birds again, but I can sing as he sang, and all who hear me will think that Othmar sings too. Rejoice, my sisters, sing and rejoice," but at that moment the dwarf started up crying out—

"The dawn, the dawn, my children; see, the sun, the sun; beware, beware its rays." Then came a great burst of sound like a chord from all the

She bent forward, and clasped him in her slender arms, and kissed him
on the lips.

music folk, followed by a flash of light like lightning, and when it had cleared away, the singing men and girls had gone, and in their places there lay upon the ground all the musical instruments—fiddles, viols, pipes, horns, and cymbals. Othmar stood staring as if he had been turned to stone, and watched as if he were in a dream, while the little man quietly packed the instruments on to the mule, and went away leading it by the bridle as he had come.

"Good-bye, Othmar," he called back, "good-bye. When you hear my fiddles again, they will be sweeter than ever, for I have added your voice to them." And he went on his way over the hill-side and disappeared beyond the ridge. Othmar ran after him, but he stumbled and fell. He tried to call out, but no voice would come! Tears ran down his cheeks, and he sobbed bitterly, but no sound came with the sobs, and he knew that his voice had left him. The singing girl had stolen it, and he could never sing or cry out again!

The sun was rising high in the heavens. The green lizards, slow-worms, frogs and beetles were still ranged around, and gazed at Othmar with

their heads wonderingly on one side. The birds
sang louder and louder, and their voices sounded
sweet in the morning air. Othmar bent his
head and wept because he knew that never could
he call them to him again. Then from behind a
bush there rose a big black raven, who cast a long
shadow behind him which almost covered Othmar

as he sat, and it gave a deep croak and then
spoke quite clearly—

"Poor Othmar!" it said, "she has stolen your
voice!" and he hopped down. "You will never
speak nor sing again. Poor Othmar!—ah! they
stole my voice too; once I could sing far better
than the birds you hear now. That was thousands

of years ago, but the dwarf came to my nest, and told me if I would go with him he would teach me how to whistle so that the worms should rise out of the ground and jump into my mouth when they heard me, and he called one of his trumpet-men to teach me—one you saw dance— and he bid me lay my beak below his lips while he sang ; then he stole my voice, all but a croak, which he did not want because it was so harsh, but all your voice was sweet, therefore she has got it all—poor Othmar, poor Othmar !"

Then Othmar raised himself, with the tears running from his eyes, and turned to find his way back to the village. It seemed a long distance, for he missed his path, and it was near nightfall before he saw the tops of the cottages and his own little home ; but as he neared the village, he could see Hulda standing in the road, shading her eyes from the sun, and watching the way he came.

"Othmar," she cried when she saw him, "is it you? I have been to search for you far and near, and there are others now looking for you, for we were afraid lest you had fallen down some crevice, or slipped over the rocks."

Othmar came up to her, and put out his hand,

and she saw how pale he was, and that his eyes were full of tears, but he said nothing.

"Othmar, tell me," cried Hulda; "what has happened? why don't you speak?" but still Othmar was silent. "Are you hurt, Othmar? Did the dwarf do you any harm?"

Then Othmar flung himself on the ground, and began to sob, but his sobs gave no sound, though the ground was wet with his tears, and Hulda knew that Othmar was dumb.

"Poor Othmar, poor Othmar!" croaked the raven who had kept close to Othmar, and flew overhead, but Hulda did not understand it, only she wept to see his grief.

"Never fear, Othmar," she said tenderly, "your voice will soon come back; it was the long cold night, and the fear that has driven it away. Come home with me, and let me nurse you, and you shall soon be well."

Othmar shook his head, and the tears fell from his eyes, but he let her take his hand and lead him into the village where his old mother sat and waited for him; but still, although she sprang forward to greet him, and put her arms around his neck, he could not speak, and his deep sobs gave no sound. At first the villagers said he was ill, and soon he would be well again, but as the days passed and he never spoke, they knew that he was struck dumb. Some said it was the cold, and some that he had been frightened; only Hulda said to herself, " it was the wicked little man."

So the days passed, and Othmar remained silent and worked with the other young men of the village without speaking, and no longer could he sing or call the birds to him. Always he looked white and sad, but saddest of all when there was any village merry-making, and the villagers sang and danced together. Then when he heard them he would put his fingers in his ears and hide his eyes so as not to see them and run afar off by himself; for the sound of any music was quite horrible to him after the singing of the travelling musicians. So a year passed, and Othmar never spoke, and instead of calling him the bird-boy, the village people called him " dumb Othmar."

It was midsummer-night, and the villagers had been having a merry-making and dancing cheerily on the green in the village. Othmar was not

with them ; he had left the village and went and
sat apart on the top of a rocky hill, from where
afar the sea could be seen when the weather was
clear.   The moon was wonderfully bright, and
the country was almost as light as by day.
Othmar could hear the sound of their laughter,
but he never laughed, and as he sat with his
head bowed upon his knees he wept silently.
So he remained alone till far into the night
when all the singing and dancing was done,
and the villagers had gone home, but just
when the clocks struck twelve he saw Hulda,
who came slowly to him, and he saw that she
too was crying.

"Othmar," she said, "I have thought and
thought, and I know that the little man with the
fiddles was a wicked fairy." Othmar nodded.
"So I am going into the big world to find him,
for if he has done you this ill he will know how
to cure you, and I have saved all my money for
a year."

Then Othmar took her hand, and kissed it,
but still wept, as he shook his head and made
signs to her that she must not go, as it would
be all in vain.   But Hulda did not heed him.

"And now," she said, "I am going, Othmar, and it may be long years before I return, so you must do three things. First, you must give me a long curl of your brown hair, that I may lay it next my heart and wear it day and night, not to forget you. Then you must kiss me on my lips to say good-bye ; and then you must promise that my name shall be the first words your lips say when they again can speak." Then Othmar took his knife and cut from his head the longest, brightest curl of his hair, and drew her to him and kissed her thrice upon the lips, and then he took her hand and with it wrote upon his lips her name, " Hulda," as a promise that her name should be the first thing they said.

"Good-bye, Othmar," she said ; "you will wait for me." Then she turned away and started alone to go down the mountain-side, and she looked back as she went and called back, " Good-bye, Othmar," as long as he could see or hear her.

She went straight down the hill and journeyed for a long way, till the dawn began to show red in the sky, and she lay under a tree and slept soundly till the sun had risen and woke her.

She sat and thought which way she should go.

"I must seek out some wise man who knows about fairies and wicked witches," she said to herself, "and who will tell me where to search. And I will ask every one I meet where the wisest person is to be found." So she went on for many days till she came to a tiny village, outside which, in a field, she saw a shepherd minding sheep. Hulda stopped and asked if he could tell her where she could find a very wise man who could answer her question.

The shepherd thought a bit, and then he said, "The wisest man in these parts lives up in the little cottage on the other side of the village. He cured my sheep two years back when all the flock were sick and many died—a little cottage with a red gate." Hulda thanked the shepherd, and went on till she came to the little cottage with the red gate. When she had knocked at the door a tall man came out, and she asked him if 'twas he who had cured the shepherd's sheep, and as he was so clever, if he would tell her what to do. She told him she wanted to find a dwarf who led a donkey covered with musical instruments, and whom she knew to be a wicked sorcerer, since he struck folk dumb.

The tall man looked at her and said, "My business is to cure sheep, cows, and horses, and I know it right well; but I know nothing of dwarfs and witches, and how can I tell you which way he has gone, or anything about him?"

"Then of whom had I best ask?" said Hulda. "Tell me who is the wisest and most learned man in these parts, and I will go to him."

The tall man rubbed his head and considered. "I suppose," quoth he, "that the old school-master at the village school yonder would be said to be the most learned man hereabouts, for he teaches the children all sorts of things that they forget when they grow up. That is the school-house on the hill." So on went Hulda again to the school.

As she came near she could hear the children calling out their lessons, and their master, who was an old priest, teaching them. So she waited about till school hours were over, and the children had all come out, and then she timidly went in and curtseyed to the old school-master, and told him her tale, and asked him, as he was so very learned, if he would advise her what to do; but instead of answering her the old man at first stared at her

in bewilderment, and then he said, " I can teach
you to read and write and many wonderful things,
but of dwarfs who can steal a boy's voice I know
nothing. You would do best not to think more
of it."

" But some one there must be," cried Hulda,
beginning to cry, "who can tell me what to do,
and which way to go. For I am sure that the
old man was a fairy, and if so, no living man
can help Othmar, but only he who did the
mischief can undo it."

The old priest looked at her sadly and shook
his head. " My child," he said, "this is a foolish
talk about fairies and sorcerers, I know nothing
of such things. It is only untaught folk and
fools who give heed to such matters."

" To untaught folk and fools then I must go, for
surely they can help me more than the wise," she
cried. So she left the school-house, and started
again through the little village street. The first
person she met was a baker going home after
taking round his bread, and she stopped him and
asked him who was the most ignorant and foolish
person in those parts.

The baker stood and stared at her, and seemed

to be half angry. At last he said, "I am sure I don't know anything about fools. You had better go on to the cake-maker, who lives a mile up the hill. He is, to my mind, the biggest fool

in these parts." And tossing his basket about and seeming to be much offended, he went his way. Hulda went on for a mile up the hill, and there she found a little group of cottages, and in their midst was a shop with an open oven, and

she could see its owner busy making cakes and
sweets.   Hulda went in and bought a cake,
and as she sat and ate it, she asked the man
timidly if he knew many of the people in that
neighbourhood, and if any were very ignorant
and foolish.

"Indeed," cried the man, "you may well ask
that. Why, a more silly, ignorant set of folk I
never knew, quite different from the people in
my native town, but that is miles away."

"And who do you think the silliest then?"
asked Hulda.

"Why, for sure 'tis hard to say," said the man,
scratching his head. "They're such a poor silly
lot, right away from the Mayor down to Tommy
the fool."

"And who is Tommy the fool?" asked Hulda
eagerly.

"'Tis a poor natural-born idiot who lives with
his mother in the little cabin on the side of the
common. He spends all his time trying to catch
a bird, and he never has caught one, and never
will."

"Thank you for telling me about him," said
Hulda, rising to go away. "Maybe if he is

really a fool he could answer my questions as they say," and she went on again with a lighter heart. At last she came to the common on which the fool lived with his mother. When she approached the little cabin, she saw some one dancing about in front of an oak, dressed up with the feathers of birds and fowls, which looked as if they had been picked up from the ground. He was a young man of about eighteen, and he had a cheerful face, but any one looking at him could see at once he was an idiot. He was dancing round the tree and pointing up to the birds, and calling them to come down to him. Hulda came up and stood quite close and watched him, as he ran round smiling and giggling. Then she said, " Please can you tell me where I shall find a little man, a dwarf who drives a donkey covered with pipes and fiddles ? "

The fool looked at her very gravely, but he said nothing ; so then she went on to tell him how the little man had come to their village, and how he had stolen Othmar's voice, and how she had come out to seek it. Just as she finished speaking, there rose from the ground a raven, and soared above their heads. When he saw it the fool pointed to it, and cried out, " The raven, the raven, follow the raven," and as the raven flew, he ran after him with Hulda following in turn. They ran for a long way, the fool leaping and bounding, and pointing with his finger and crying, " The raven, the raven, do what the raven does." Then suddenly he turned, giving a wild laugh, and began to run home again, but as he went he nodded and called to Hulda, " Follow the raven, follow it, do what the raven does."

Hulda felt inclined to burst into tears with disappointment, but still she ran meekly after the bird, murmuring to herself, " He said follow the raven, but what good can that do me?" But when the fool had turned back, the raven slackened his pace, and cawed and lighted on a tree, and Hulda, panting for breath, sat down under it, and looked up at it.

" Poor Hulda!" it croaked, but she couldn't understand it; "poor Hulda, come with me, and I will show you where the dwarf is." Then it began to fly slowly on again.

"What shall I do?" sobbed Hulda. " He was only an idiot, he knew nothing; still he told me to follow the raven, and no one else has told me anything;" so on she went, and this time the raven flew quite slowly, so that Hulda kept up with it walking. On they travelled till evening was well advanced, into all sorts of places where Hulda had never been, and through many villages. Then it began to grow dark, and the moon came out, but still they travelled on. Hulda was footsore and weary, but she would not give up, and said to herself, " It was what the fool said, ' Follow the raven, do what the raven does !' "

Just before dawn, they came out on to a big plain, where there were neither houses nor trees, but in the far distance you could see a long line of mountains ; a little further in the centre of the plain Hulda saw a little dark mass, and straight to this the raven flew, and as Hulda approached it, she saw that it was the little dwarf, lying asleep upon the ground beside his heap of musical instruments, with the mule grazing near. "Oh, good wise fool," cried Hulda, "now indeed you have given me the best advice. Since the raven has led me to the wicked dwarf, now indeed will I do what the raven does, whatever it be."

The raven flew on, and lit upon a scrubby bush,

a little way from the sleeping dwarf, and Hulda followed and crouched beside it, making no noise lest she should disturb the sleeper, and hiding behind the branches so that she could not be seen. Presently the little man rose from the ground, and called out, "Come, my children, practice, practice ; the dawn is here, and the sun will rise, and then we must go upon our way."

Then Hulda saw what Othmar had seen before. The pipes raised themselves from the ground, and untwisted, and became tall, lithe men ; some gradually uncurled themselves, and put forth long arms and became beautiful girls, till each instrument had taken the likeness of a human being. Then they began to dance and to sing, and Hulda watched them as Othmar had watched them, and she too felt as if she had never seen and heard anything so beautiful in her life, and she longed to rush to them, but she heard the raven croak above her, and remembered the words of the fool, "The raven, the raven, do what the raven does." Then she saw that the raven had hopped off the tree, and was standing upon the earth in front of her, and was beginning to dig in the earth with its long beak, as if it would find a worm. "The fool said, Do what the raven does, so must I dig too," thought she, and she began to scoop the brown earth with her hand, till she had made a hole, watching the raven all the time.

Presently she saw that the raven had found a long worm, and held it by its throat in the air, but it did not swallow it. Hulda looked into her hole to see if there was a worm there also, and at the bottom she saw lying a long, lithe, green snake, twisted up and apparently torpid. "Surely," thought Hulda, "if I do what the raven does, I shall take this out," and she put her hand into the hole, and grasped the snake by its throat, though she was very much afraid of it, and then she crouched down behind the raven and the bush.

"Come," cried the dwarf, when they had all sung together, "now let us hear the last new voice. Othmar's voice was as sweet as silver. Now let me hear how my youngest daughter has treated it." Then there came to the front the youngest and fairest of the girls, and began to sing, and when she heard it, Hulda could scarcely keep from screaming, for she recognized that the tones were Othmar's; but just as the singing sounded the sweetest, the raven with a croak opened his

mouth, and dropped the worm upon the ground,
and Hulda let go her hold of the bright green
snake, which darted through the short grass
towards the dancers.

There arose from all sides the cry of " A snake,
a snake!" and they seemed panic-stricken. The
snake glided straight towards the singing girl, and
deftly coiled itself round her ankles, while from
the old man and all the others came a terrible
uproar, but the snake from the girl's ankles had
slid up her body in bright green coils, and then
twisted itself around her throat, and coiled tighter
and tighter and tighter, till her head fell over
on one side. Then Hulda heard a noise like
the sighing of wind, but sweet and tender, while
the dwarf and all the singers were in a hubbub
and confusion.

For a moment the old man stood motionless,
then he rose and gave a terrible cry. Hulda
trembled when she heard his voice, it sounded
like nothing earthly, but ere he was silent there
had risen from the ground and from the bushes
near a number of little cloudy forms, black and
thick, and twirling in all directions, and they
twisted in and out among the singers ; and as

they twisted among them, they ceased to be men and women, but became musical instruments, as they had been before, all save the girl around whose neck the snake had wound, and who seemed to shrivel and shrivel in its coils till she was no more to be seen.

In less than a minute they were all packed again upon the mule, and the little old man was leading it quietly away, as if nothing had happened. And upon the grass lay the glittering snake, though all trace of the girl around whose neck it had twisted had gone. Hulda ran to it, and then she almost cried, for she feared that after all the girl with Othmar's voice had escaped her. But she remembered the words of Tommy the fool, " Do as the raven does ; follow the raven," and looking up she saw that the raven was fluttering above her, with the worm it had picked up from the ground in its mouth.

"Oh, dear raven," cried Hulda, "you brought me to where the little man was, now lead me back and show me what to do next." And mindful of the fool's advice, she picked up the snake, and holding it firmly by the throat, turned to follow the raven, who flew ahead of her. Thus they journeyed back, over the same country through which Hulda had come before. All looked just the same, but Hulda was sorely tired, for she had now been walking many days, and she felt sad, for she did not know if after all she had gained anything, or whether she ought not to have followed the little old man, and though she had heard Othmar's voice, she did not know how she was to get it back to him. " Never mind," she said to herself, "the fool told me right so far, and evidently he knew all about it, so I had best keep to his advice."

The sun rose high in the sky and the day was very hot, and poor Hulda longed to lie down under the trees and sleep; moreover the snake in her hand twisted and twisted, till she could scarce hold it. Sometimes she cried from very weariness, but still the raven flew in front of her. She had bought dry bread as she came along, and when the raven stopped and hopped upon the ground, she munched it to stave off her hunger, but directly the raven began to fly she followed it, and she never let the snake from her grasp. The sun had set, and dark was all over the land ere she came to the village where the fool lived, but

no fool was there to be seen. Hulda sought
everywhere, but she could not find him. Then
she saw that the raven had stopped and settled
on the roof of the cottage where the fool lived,
and, standing on one leg, had gone to sleep with
its head under its wing, so Hulda lay down by
the side of the door, and laying her head on a
stone rested too. But first she took off her girdle
and tied it firmly round the snake's throat, and
then tied it round her waist again lest she should
fall asleep and the snake glide away.

Just when the stars were beginning to look pale,
and as there were signs of the dawn in the sky, the
door of the cottage opened, and out there came
the fool, dressed up as Hulda had seen him before,
with feathers and weeds and bits of bright rag.
Hulda started up, and he laughed when he saw
her. "Look," he said, "the sun is rising; I am
come out to see it."

"I have come back," cried Hulda, "and I have
seen them all—the old man and the musician girls,
and the one who stole Othmar's voice will never
use it again, for this snake has throttled her; but
what am I to do now? How can I give him back
his voice? What shall I do to make him speak?"

And as she spoke she took the snake from her
bosom and showed it to the fool. He looked at
it very gravely as he always did when anything
was shown to him, and looked very wise and
nodded. "It is a snake," he said; "perhaps
Othmar will like the snake."

Hulda begged him to tell her if he knew what
she should do, but he would say no more, but
began to dance and sing as she had seen him
do before. Then at last Hulda burst out crying,
"He is nothing but a poor idiot," she said, "and
I have been on a fool's errand when I did as he
told me, though I did see the wicked little man,
and this snake did punish the singing girl, so I
will take it back to Othmar that he may see I
have tried. But now I believe he will be dumb
for ever."

And she took the snake and looked at it as she
held it. It was very still, and seemed half torpid,
though the weather was warm. She saw it was
not a common snake, for it was bright brown, and
green with odd markings, and it glittered oddly
when the sun's rays touched it.

"I will go back now," said Hulda; "I will go
back to Othmar, and tell him I have failed, and

ask him to forgive my vanity in thinking I could help him. I will go back at once and tell him all." And overhead the raven croaked and told her to go quickly, but she did not understand what he said.

So again she began to trudge on, holding the snake in her hands and toiling over fields and moors in the way that she knew led to her own little village, though by now her feet were so swollen and her legs so stiff that she almost cried for pain.

Presently she came to the village where the cake-maker lived, and as she passed his shop, she saw that he stood at the door and nodded to her as he saw her coming.

"Good-day," he cried; "you are the young wench I saw go past awhile back."

"Yes, I am going home now," said Hulda.

"And have you found your fiddles and horns that turned to men and women?" he asked. "It was a fool's errand, I fear, you were going on; and what have you got in your hand now?"

"It is a snake," answered Hulda, "and——"

"A snake!" screamed the cake-maker. "Lord love the girl, is she mad to go wandering over the

country carrying a snake with her ? Why, it might
kill you, wench ! Drop it at once ! "

" No, indeed, I will not drop it," said Hulda,
"for it seems to me that it is the only thing
which may do Othmar good, for at any rate it
has killed the girl who stole his voice, and——"

At this the man started and called out, " Good
Lord, she is clean off her head. Stolen Othmar's
voice ! What can the wench mean ? Why, girl,
that snake might bite you, and you would be dead
at once. Why on earth should you carry it because
it has killed a girl ? "

" I am carrying it because the fool told me to
do what the raven does," answered Hulda, " and
he has still a worm in his mouth. Look."

At this the man burst out laughing. " Why,
what has that to do with you ? " he cried ; "a
raven will often carry a worm for a bit. Drop
this snake at once, you silly lass, or, better still,
hold it firm while I crush its head with my poker."
And he seized the poker to kill it with.

Then Hulda was frightened lest he might steal
the snake from her, or kill it by force, and she
ran on ; but she ran in such haste that she
stumbled against the baker who was just coming

out from his shop with his basket of loaves on his arm.

"Can't you look where you are going?" he cried in anger, as he picked up the bread which had rolled into the road ; and then, seeing it was Hulda, he said :—"Why, who are you running away from, my girl? Are you on the look-out for more fools that you can't see when an honest man comes along? And whatever have you got there?"

"It is only a snake I have found," said Hulda, when she had asked the man's pardon, and she tried to hide the snake in her skirt, but the baker seized her arm and made her show it to him.

"What on earth are you carrying a live snake with you for?" he asked. "Don't you know they are venomous beasts, and the bite of one is certain death?" And, like the cake-maker, he tried to wrench the snake from her. At this Hulda was terribly frightened.

"If they take the snake from me," she thought, "then my last chance is gone," and she tried to free herself from the baker, but he seized her by the skirt and held her fast, and shouted out to others to come and help him.

" Help, help ! " he cried. " Here is a poor mad girl, and she has got hold of a poisonous adder, and she will let it loose in the village and it will bite some of our children and kill them." And when they heard his cry the villagers all came running out of their cottages.

" Let me go, let me go," shrieked Hulda, " it will do no harm. I will hold it tight, and I would not lose it for the wide world."

" I tell you she is mad," roared the baker, and the cake-maker came up and said the same thing. " She wandered by here some time back, and all she wanted to know was where she could find another as mad as herself, but she will have far to go before she meets one, I reckon. We must secure her and take the snake from her, but beware how you catch it, for fear it should bite."

And the people all gathered round her and made a great hubbub, though they were afraid to touch the snake which Hulda still held firmly in her hand. And they made such a din that the old school-master came out of the school-house with his pupils after him.

The people told him there was a poor mad girl who had got a snake, and would not let

them take it from her, and he remembered Hulda
as the others had done, and shook his head and
said sadly, " I fear it is too true. The poor child
is really mad, but we cannot wrench the snake
from her lest it may turn and bite us. But it is
certain that it would not be safe to let her go ;
so, as the children are all going home now, let
us lock her into the school-house here, till we
can get something to kill the creature with, and
then when the doctor comes, he can see if the
poor girl is very bad, and what had better be
done with her."

Hulda turned quite white with fear, and cried
out that she was not mad, and that the snake
should harm no one, but they would not heed her,
and pushed her into the school-house, and bolted
the doors on her, and there Hulda sat on the
floor and cried as if her heart would break.

" Alas ! " cried she, " now all hope is gone, and
Othmar will be dumb for ever. For what good
have I carried this snake with me all this way,
if now it is to be taken from me and killed ? " and
her tears fell on the viper as she looked at it in
her hand. It was very bright green and yellow,
and it kept wrinkling and twisting its skin as she

grasped it, and making a loud hissing noise. As her tears were still falling she heard a croak over her head, and saw the raven perched on a window above her, and again her hopes revived.

" Maybe he has come to help me," she thought, " for I should never have found the little dwarf if it had not been for the raven." Then as she looked up at the raven sitting in the window, she saw that it was pecking at a piece of rope that hung through the window, and Hulda thought —" Surely if I could climb up to the window, I could scramble through it, and climb down the rope on to the ground. Only if they were to see me, they would catch me again, so I must wait till nightfall when there is no one there."

So she sat down again and waited till the sun had set, and she trembled at every noise lest it might be some one coming to seek her, but they left her alone, and no one came. When it was quite dark, and all the village was quiet she went to the window, and tried to climb up to it, but she found that she could not manage to get up on to the window-sill while she held the snake in her hand. Then first she thought she would wind it around her waist, but she remembered how it had tightened around the singing girl and killed her, and for some time she could not think what to do with it. At last she twisted it into a knot, and placed it in her bosom, though she trembled lest it should bite her. And when she placed it in her bosom, she saw the curl of Othmar's hair that lay there, and she took it and tied up the snake's jaws with it so that it might not open its mouth. " For Othmar's hair will not break or give way," she said ; " it is like his heart, it will be true and strong till the end."

Then she climbed up on to the window-ledge, and scrambled through the window, and took the piece of rope and let herself down on to the ground outside. And when she lit upon the ground, she heard the raven croaking above her, and her heart leapt for joy, and she began to run as fast as she could to get away from the village lest they might catch her again.

When she came again into the open country, she looked for the raven, and saw that it was flying in front of her as before, towards the distant mountains where she knew lay her home. She toiled on, for many days, but by now the summer had nearly passed away, and when she got into the high mountain land, she found that the cold winter had given signs of coming, and the trees were beginning to be bare, and there was a light white frost on the ground. It was far into the night when she arrived in the village, and the villagers were all asleep and their cottages shut. Outside the cottage where Othmar lived grew a big old ivy tree, and on this the raven perched, and underneath it Hulda lay down to wait the dawn and Othmar's waking. She lay quiet for a bit, but when she saw a faint glimmering of light where the sun was going to rise, she felt she could be still no longer, and she sprang up and called, " Othmar, come down, I am here," for she dreaded having to tell him before the other villagers that she had failed.

In a few moments the door of the cottage opened and Othmar came out, and ran to greet her, but she kept afar.

" Othmar," she cried, " I have done you no good, save that I have punished the wicked girl who took your voice. This snake killed her, so she will never sing as you did again. See." And she held out the snake to him ; it was curled round and still tied up with his hair, and as the sun began to shine it glittered brightly.

" But I have done you no good, indeed rather harm," Hulda went on, "for I have made you hope where there was no hope, and you have waited and expected that I should bring you back what you had lost, and I have not done it, and now I shall never hear you say my name ' Hulda ' again," and she wept so bitterly that the tears fell from her face, and dropped upon the snake which still she grasped. Othmar held out his hand, and tried to take her hand that he might kiss it, and as he did so, he touched the snake's long tail, and it began to writhe and twist, and glisten more and more as the sun shone on it. And as he raised her hand to his mouth, Othmar tried to say her name " Hulda " with his poor dumb lips that could make no sound, and he breathed it on the snake, and it seemed as if the snake vibrated with the name, and suddenly it swelled and swelled, and shone still more brightly, and its mouth grew wide and burst Othmar's hair which had bound it, and widened out till it was not a snake any more, but a curled golden trumpet, curled up as the snake had been, and like that which had been changed into the singing girl who stole Othmar's voice. "Take it, Othmar, and blow," cried Hulda, and he put it to his lips and cried "Hulda!" and Hulda heard her name echoing back in a burst of music from all around. At its sound the birds awoke in all the trees, and began their morning chorus, and the village folk ran to their windows to see what the trumpet's peal had been, and saw Othmar standing with Hulda in his arms, and at their feet the bright trumpet which he had dropped. It lay on the ground, but as Othmar began to speak and to say, "Hulda, Hulda, you have brought it back, you have given me my voice again," the trumpet broke into many pieces, and with every word crumbled, till there was nothing left but a little heap of shining golden sand, and from under it there glided out a dark green snake with yellow markings, and it slid away into the bushes and disappeared.

Then all the villagers rejoiced, and Hulda wept with happiness. And Othmar married Hulda, and his voice never left him again; but when long years after folk would tell him his voice was

sweet and far more beautiful than the birds, he
would say, " But it is not really my voice, it is
my wife's, Hulda's, for I should have been dumb
for ever if she had not sought it and brought it
back to me."

THE RAIN MAIDEN

NCE upon a time there lived a shepherd and his wife, who lived in a very lonely little cottage far from town or village, near some mountains. It was a wild neighbourhood, and the wind blew across the mountains fiercely, and the rain often fell so heavily that it seemed as if the cottage would be washed away. One evening when the shepherd was out, there came on a great storm of rain which beat against the doors and the windows violently. As the shepherd's wife sat listening to it by the fire, it seemed to her as if it sounded

192

louder than she had ever heard it before, and the raindrops sounded like the knock of a hand that was knocking to gain admittance. It went on for a little time, till the shepherd's wife could bear to listen to it no longer, and she rose and went to the door to open it, though she knew that she would let the wind and rain into the room. As she opened the door a gust of rain was blown in her face, and then she saw that in the doorway stood a woman who had been knocking. She was a tall woman wrapped in a grey cloak with long hair falling down her back. " Thank you," she said. And though her voice was very low, the shepherd's wife could hear it plainly through all the storm. " Thank you for opening the door to me. Many would have let me stand outside. Now may I come into your cottage and rest ? "

" How wet you must be ! " cried the shepherd's wife ; " come in and rest, and let me give you food. Have you come from far ? "

" No, I come from quite near," said the woman, and she came into the cottage as she spoke, and sat down in a chair near the door. " And I want no food, only a glass of water. I must go on

o

directly, but I have not far to go, and I shall be no wetter than I am now."

The shepherd's wife stared in surprise, for she saw that apparently the woman's clothes were not wet at all. And what was stranger still, though she had thought she was only clad in a dull grey cloak, now she saw that she was covered with jewellery,—clear stones, like diamonds with many flashing colours ; and she also saw that all her clothes were of the finest. She gave her a glass of water, and begged that as well she might give her other food, but the woman shook her head, and said no, water was all she needed. When she had drunk the water she gave back the glass to the shepherd's wife, and said, " And so this is your home. Have you all that you want in life? Are you happy ? "

" Ay, we are happy enough," said the shepherd's wife, " save indeed for one thing. Ten years ago my little baby girl died, and I have no other children. I long for one sorely, that I might take care of it and make it happy, while it is little, and then in turn, when I am old, it would love and care for me.'

" And if you had a little child," said the woman,

rising up and standing before the shepherd's wife, "you think you would really love it better than anything in the world. Many women say that, but few do it. Before long a little child will be born to you, and as long as you love it better than anything in the world it will remain with you, but when you love anything else better than your little daughter and her happiness, it will go from you ; so remember my words. Good-bye," and the woman walked to the door and went quietly out into the rain, and the shepherd's wife saw her disappearing, and the rain pelting around her, but her clothes were not blown about, neither did the rain seem to wet her.

A year passed away, and the shepherd's wife had a tiny daughter, a lovely little baby with the bluest eyes and the softest skin ; the evening she was born the wind howled and the rain fell as fiercely as on the night when the grey woman had come into the shepherd's cottage. The shepherd and his wife both loved their little daughter very dearly, as well they might, as no fairer child was ever seen. But as she grew older, some things about her frightened her mother, and she had some ways of which she could not cure

her. She would never go near a fire, however
cold she was, neither did she love the sunshine,
but always ran from it and crept into the shade ;
but when she heard the rain pattering against the
window-panes she would cry, " Listen, mother,
listen to my brothers and sisters dancing," and
then she would begin to dance too in the cottage

her little feet pattering upon the boards ; or, if she
possibly could, she would run out on to the moor
and dance, with the rain falling upon her, and her
mother had much ado to get her to come back
into the cottage, yet she never seemed to get very
wet, nor did she catch cold. A river ran near the
cottage, and by it she would go and sit for hours

dabbling her feet in the water, and singing sweet
little songs to herself. Still, in all other ways she
was a good, affectionate girl, and did all that her
mother told her, and seemed to love both her

parents tenderly, and the shepherd's wife would
say to herself, " My only trouble is that when she
is grown up, she will want to marry, and leave me,
and I shall have to do without her." Time passed,

and the old shepherd died, but his wife and daughter still lived on in the little cottage, and the daughter grew to be a most beautiful young maiden.   Her eyes were clear light-blue, like the colour of the far-off sea, but it was difficult to say

what was the colour of her hair, save that it was very light, and hung in heavy masses over her brow and shoulders.   Once or twice her mother felt sorely frightened about her; it was when spring showers were falling, and the young girl had gone into the little garden in front of the cottage to let the rain fall upon her head and face, as she loved to do, in spite of all her mother could say. Then she began to dance, as she always did when the rain fell, and as she danced the sun came out while the rain was yet falling. Her mother watched her from the cottage-window, but while she watched her it seemed to her as if her daughter was covered with jewels of every colour, clear and bright ; they hung around her in chains, and made her look more like a king's daughter than a shepherd's girl. " Come in, child, come in," called the shepherd's wife, and when the young girl came in the cottage all traces of the jewels had gone, and when her mother upbraided her for going out to dance in the rain, she only answered, " It hurts no one, my mother, and it pleases me, why should you stop me ? "

A little way from the cottage on the mountain side stood an old castle, where formerly the Kings of the land used to come and stay, but which now had not been used for very many years. One day, however, the shepherd's wife saw great preparations were being made to beautify and adorn it, and she knew that the King and his son were coming to stay there again. Soon after they had arrived, the shepherd's daughter went down to the river, as was her wont, and sat on the bank, dipping her feet in the ripples. Presently there came up a boat, and it was a grand young man dressed all in velvet and gold who leaned over the side to fish.

" Who are you, and what are you doing here ? " cried the shepherd's daughter, for she was afraid of no one.

" I am the King's son," said he, "and I am coming here to fish. Who are you, and where do you come from, for I have never seen such a beautiful maiden in my life ? " and he looked at her and could scarce speak, so beautiful did she seem to him.

" It is cruel to take the fishes out of the water," cried the shepherd's daughter, " leave them alone, and come and dance on the bank with me," and she went under the shade of a large tree, and began to dance, and the King's son watched her, and again he thought so beautiful a maid there had never been.

Day after day he came down to the river to fish, and day after day he left the line and tackle to sit and watch the shepherd's daughter, and each

"Leave the fishes alone, and come and dance on the bank with me."

time found her more enchanting. Once he tried to kiss her hand, but she sprang from him and left him sitting in his boat alone. At last a day came when the Prince said to his father, " My father, you want me to wed so that I may have an heir to the throne, but there is only one woman that can ever be my wife, and that is the daughter of the poor woman who lives in the little cottage out yonder."

At first the old King was very wroth, but he loved his son well, and knew that nothing would shake him from his word, so he told him that if he would bring home his bride, he too would rejoice and love her as his daughter even though she be a beggar-maid. Then the young Prince rode down to the cottage, and went in and told the shepherd's wife how he had seen her daughter, and loved her and wished to make her his wife, so that she would be Queen of the country.

The shepherd's wife went nearly wild with joy. "To think that my daughter should be the Queen," she said to herself, and when her daughter came into the cottage she did not know how to contain herself, but folded her in her arms and kissed her, crying and declaring that never was woman so blessed.

" Why, what has happened, my mother ? and what has pleased you so ? " said her daughter, while still the shepherd's wife rejoiced and wept for joy.

" It is the King's son, my girl, the King's own son, and he has just been here, and he loves you because you are so beautiful, and he will marry you and make you Queen of all the land. Was there ever such luck for a poor woman ? "

But the daughter only said, " But I don't want to marry the King's son, mother, or any one. I will never be the wife of any man ; I will stay with you and nurse you when you are old and sick, for I can live in no house but this cottage, and have no friend but my mother."

On hearing this the shepherd's wife became very angry, and told her daughter that she must be mad, and that she must wait for a day or two, and she would be only too thankful for the love of the King's son, and for the honour he was going to do her in making her his Queen. But still the daughter shook her head, and said quite quietly, " I will never be the wife of the King's son."

The shepherd's wife did not dare tell the King's son what her daughter had said, but told him that he had better speak to her himself if he wished to make her his wife. Then when he was again sitting in the boat on the river, and the maiden on the bank, the King's son told her how much he loved her, and that he would share with her all that he had in this world. But the shepherd's daughter only shook her head and said, " I will never live at the palace, and I will never be a Queen."

The old King had ordered great preparations to be made for the wedding, which was to take place immediately, and all sorts of fine clothes were ordered for the shepherd's daughter, that she might appear properly as the wife of the Prince, but for the few days just before the wedding, the rain fell as it had never been known to have fallen ; it beat through the roofs of the cottages, and the river swelled and overflowed its banks; everyone was frightened, save indeed the shepherd's daughter, who went out into the wet and danced as was her wont, letting the torrents fall upon her head and shoulders.

But the evening before the wedding-day she

knelt beside her mother's side. "Dear mother,"
she said, "let me stop with you and nurse you
when you are old. Do not send me away to the
palace to live with the King's son."

Then the mother was very angry, and told her
daughter that she was very ungrateful, and she
ought to be thankful that such luck had come in
her way, and who was she, the daughter of a poor
shepherd, that she should object to marrying the
King's son ?

All night long the rain fell in torrents, and
when next day the shepherd's daughter was
dressed in all her finery, it was through pools on
the ground that she had to step into the grand
carriage which the King had sent to fetch her, and
while the marriage-service was being read, the
priest's voice could scarcely be heard for the
pattering of the drops upon the roof, and when
they went into the castle to the banquet, the water
burst through the doors opened to receive them,
so that the King and the wedding guests had hard
ado to keep dry. It was a grand feast, and the
King's son sat at one end of the table, and his
young wife was beside him dressed in white and
gold. All the courtiers and all the fine guests

declared that surely the world had never contained such a beautiful young woman as their future Queen. But just when the goblets were filled with wine, to drink to the health of the bride and bridegroom, there came a cry, " The floods! the floods!" and the servants ran into the hall, crying out that the waters were pouring in, and in one moment the rooms were filled with water, and no one thought of anything but to save themselves. When the hurricane had subsided, and the waters gone down, they looked around for the Prince's wife, who was nowhere to be found. Every one said that she had been swept away by the torrents, and that she had been drowned in all her youth and beauty; only the shepherd's wife wept alone, and remembered the words of the woman who came to her on the night of the storm: " When you love aught on earth better than your daughter and her happiness, she will go from you."

The King's son mourned his wife, and for long would not be comforted; but when many years had passed, he married a beautiful Princess, and with her lived very happily; only when the rain fell in torrents and beat against the window-panes it would seem to him as if he heard the sound of dancing feet, and a voice that called out, "Come and dance with me, come and dance with me and my brothers and sisters, oh, King's son, and feel our drops upon your face."

A YOUNG ploughman was following his plough in a field one morning when suddenly the horses stopped, and do what he would he could not make them stir. Then he tried to push the plough himself, but he could not move it one hair's - breadth. He stooped down to see what could be stopping it, when a deep voice cried, "Stop, I am coming up." The voice was so loud that the plough-

man shook with fear, but though he looked all around him, he could see no one from whom it could come. But presently it spoke again (only this time it was a little lower), and called out, " Have patience, and I shall be up in a moment." The ploughman quaked in every limb, and stood quite still, and the voice began again (but this time it was no louder than most folks'), and it said—" If you will only not be in such a hurry, I will tell you what I want. Look in front of your horse's right foot, and pick me up."

He bent down and looked on the ground, and there in the earth, just in front of his horse's right foot, he saw what he thought was a little black lizard. He touched it very cautiously, and started back with surprise when the voice spoke again, and he found it came from this tiny creature.

"Yes," it said, " that is quite right. You can pick me up in your hand if you like, but I think I must grow a little bigger, as I am really uncomfortably small," and while he held it on the palm of his hand, the ploughman saw that it was beginning to grow larger, and it swelled so fast that in a few seconds it was near a foot high, and he had to take both hands to hold it. Then he saw that it was not a lizard, but a little black woman with a face that looked as though it were made of india-rubber, and ugly little black hands.

" There, that will do," said the strange little gnome. " That is a nice useful size. Oh dear, how tiring growing is! I don't think I'll be any bigger just yet. Now be sure you don't drop me, and handle me very carefully, for I do not like to be roughly touched. I have not slept nearly as long as I meant to. I wanted a hundred years' nap, and it cannot be more than fifty, but now that I am awake I think I will keep so for a bit. You seem to be rather a nice civil young man. How would you like to take me for a lodger ? "

" A lodger ! " gasped the ploughman. " Why, what should I do with you ? "

" I should give no trouble," said the gnome. " But are there any women in your house ? "

" No," said the ploughman, " for I have no wife, and I am too poor to keep a servant."

" So much the better," said the gnome. " For though I am a woman myself, I detest women, and only get on with men."

"You a woman!" cried the ploughman, and he laughed outright.

" Of course I am a woman," said the creature. " Come, say quickly, do you like to have me for a lodger or not ?   Of course you will have to agree to my terms."

"And what are your terms?" asked the ploughman.

" Only this.   Whatever comes into the house, you must always give the best of it to me.   I will choose where I shall live for myself, when I see the house, but of all the food you have, you must save the best and give it to me.   Not much of it, but the very best pieces.   As you are a man I cannot wear your clothes, but you can give me some of their material, and of everything else that comes into the house of any sort, tobacco, or carpets, or furniture, I must have some of the best.   And at meals I must always be helped first.   If you agree to this, I may stay with you for a very long time."

"Oh, oh," said the ploughman, " and pray what shall I get by it ?   It seems to me as if you wanted to get the best of everything and give nothing in return."

"On the contrary," replied the gnome, "I shall give a very great deal. For as long as I remain in your house, all things will go well with you. You are a poor man now, but you will soon be a rich one. If you sow seeds they will give twice as much crop as other people's. All your animals will do well, and in a little time, instead of being a poor ploughman, you will be the richest farmer in the countryside."

"Well," quoth the ploughman, "I don't mind trying. I think it would rather amuse me to take you to my cottage ; but if you don't keep your part of the bargain, and I don't find things are going very well with me, I warn you I'll pretty soon turn you out."

"Agreed," said the gnome ; "but remember, if you fail in your compact with me, I shall go by myself. Now carry me home and let me choose where I will live."

The ploughman carried the odd little figure back to his cottage, gaping with astonishment ; there he put it down on the kitchen-table in the little kitchen. It looked all round it, and twisted about its little black head.

"That will do nicely," it said at last ; "there is

a little hole in that corner, down which I can go, and near that hole you must place all your daintiest bits, and remember that I must always be helped first at all your meals " And without a word it leaped from the table, and scuttled away down a big hole that the rats had made, and was no more to be seen.

But when in the evening the ploughman came in to eat his meal, before he began it he took the very best bit of meat and the nicest of the vegetable, and laid them down near the hole. Then he watched eagerly to see what would happen, but while he looked there they remained. Suddenly, however, the door shut with a bang, and he turned his head for a moment to see what caused it, and when he looked back the food had disappeared. Every day it was much the same. He put some of the best food on the table down near the hole, but as long as he watched there it remained, but when he took his eyes off for a moment it had disappeared. In the same way when he had new clothes, he took a choice bit of material and laid it near the hole, and it vanished also. And of whatever came into the house he took some of the best and did the same with it.

Meantime things began to improve very much with him. He had only a little bit of land round his cottage, but this year the vegetables and fruit he had planted there grew so well that he had a large quantity to send to market, and he sold them for such good prices, that soon he was able to get more land and buy his own animals, and in a little while had a farm of his own, and had grown to be quite a rich man, while all his neighbours said his luck was extraordinary. Meantime he saw or heard nothing more of the little black gnome, and except when he put the food and other things near the hole almost forgot all about her.

Time passed, and the time came when the ploughman began to think he would like to take a wife ; he made up his mind to marry a very pretty girl in the next village, who was said to be the prettiest girl in all the neighbourhood. Many of the young men would have liked to marry her, but the ploughman was a handsome, cheery young fellow, and she preferred him to all of the others, and so they were married, and she came home to live at the farm. The evening after their wedding they had a fine fat fowl for supper, and the plough-

man before he helped his wife cut off the choicest
slice from the breast and took it as usual to the
hole.

" Husband," cried the wife, " have you gone
mad that you should give the best of the food to
the rats and the mice ? "

" I am not mad at all," said the ploughman,
"but my grandfather loved nothing in the world
so well as rats and mice, and he made me promise
before he died that they should always be well
cared for in my house, and have of the best."

" Then if you are not mad," replied the wife,
" I think your grandfather was ! It is only the
best poison that is good for rats and mice, and
they shall have it soon, now that I am in the
house." But the ploughman caressed his wife and
begged her to let him keep his promise to his
grandfather, and the wife held her peace, not
liking to seem bad-tempered on her wedding-day.
After a bit she got used to her husband putting
down little bits of food, as he said, for the rats
and mice, and though she always declared she
was going to poison them, she did not try to
do so, as her husband seemed grieved when she
talked about it.

Thus things went on very happily for some months, when the wife began to think that her clothes were getting very old, and that she must have some new ones. So she took plenty of money and went into the neighbouring town, and came home with new dresses, and hats, and bonnets, and very pretty she looked in them, and her husband was very much pleased with them. But that evening after his wife was gone to bed, as the ploughman was finishing his pipe in the kitchen, he suddenly heard a deep voice from the hole, which called out just as it had done months before, "Stop, I am coming up."

For an instant the ploughman quaked with fear, then he saw something no bigger than a black beetle creeping through the hole, and it came in front of his chair, and he heard the voice, which was not so loud this time, say—

"That will do, now I am going to begin to grow a little," and it began to grow, and grow, and grow, till it was about eight inches high, and the ploughman saw it was the little black woman. "There," she said, speaking quite quietly, "that is a nice useful size, that will do. Now I have something to say to you, and you will have to attend very carefully.   I consider that you are breaking your compact.   In the first place, you married without asking my leave, and, as I told you, I don't like women in the house, but I will say nothing about that, as we had not spoken about it before, but how can you explain about all the fine clothes that your wife fetched home to-day?   She has taken them to her room and not given one to me!"

"Nay," cried the ploughman, "they are my wife's clothes, not mine."

"Nonsense," said the gnome, "you gave her the money for them.   Now understand that whatever she buys for herself in the future, she must buy the same for me.   Two of everything: dresses, hats, gloves, whatever she has, I must have too, and be sure that mine are quite as good as hers."

"But how am I to manage that?" cried the ploughman; "how can I explain it to her without telling her that you are there?"

"That is your business," said the gnome.   "All I say is that I must have the things if I am to remain in your house.   You can tell her what you please.   So now you know, and see that you do as I tell you," and suddenly the little figure shrunk up till it was about the size of a black beetle, and then disappeared down the hole without another word.

The ploughman rubbed his head, and wondered what he could do. He did not at all want to tell his wife about the little gnome, for he was sure she would not like it, but at the same time he did not want the gnome to leave his house and take away his luck.

A few days after, his wife told him she was going to the shoemaker's to buy herself some smart new shoes, and the ploughman thought of the gnome, and knew he must do as she had told him. So he said to his wife, "Wife, when you get those shoes for yourself, I wish you would get a pair just like them for my cousin who has written to me to ask me for a present. I should like to send her some nice boots and shoes as she is very poor, so I shall be very much obliged if you will get two pairs of whatever you may get for yourself that I may send her one."

The wife wondered very much, for she did not know the ploughman had any cousin; however, she went into the town, and brought home two pairs of smart red shoes with bows on the top.

When she had gone to bed at night, the ploughman took one pair and laid it by the hole in the
same place where he had put the food, and it
disappeared just as the food did without his seeing
where it went. " Now," thought he, " when she
sees I am quite honest, perhaps the ugly little
gnome will be content, and let us go on in peace."

So time went on, and the ploughman and his
wife lived very happily and quietly, till one
evening a pedlar came round with a tray holding
all sorts of pretty things to sell. The ploughman's wife went to the door, and looked at the
things : then she bought a pretty comb for her
hair, but she would not show it to her husband,
as she meant to wear it before him as a surprise
next day.

But that evening after his wife had gone to
bed, as the ploughman sat finishing his pipe by
the fire, he heard the voice from the hole calling
as loudly as ever, "Stop! I am coming up."
Again the ploughman quaked with fear, and then
he saw coming through the hole something no
bigger than a black beetle, and again the voice
said in a lower tone, " Now I will begin to grow
a little," and presently the tiny black thing had

swelled into the ugly little black woman with the face like india-rubber,

"Listen to me," she said, "and know that I am beginning to feel very angry. You are beginning to cheat me. To-day your wife bought herself a brand-new comb from a pedlar at the door, and never got one for me. To-morrow evening I must have that comb. I don't care how you get it, but have it I must."

The ploughman scratched his head and was sore perplexed. "What on earth am I to do?" he cried, "for my wife will think me very cruel if I take away all the pretty little things she buys for herself."

"I can't help that," answered the gnome. "I have got to have that comb by this time to-morrow night, and I warn you if you begin to deceive me, just as if I were an ordinary human being, I shall pretty soon take myself off," and with that the gnome disappeared through the hole in an instant.

Next morning at breakfast the wife came down with the new comb in her hair, and said to her husband, "See, husband, I bought this of the pedlar yesterday, and he tells me they are quite the newest fashion, and all the great ladies in town are wearing them."

"Well," quoth the ploughman, "such a fashion may be all very well for the great ladies who have scarce any hair of their own, but, for my own part, I had rather see your beautiful hair just as it is without any adornment."

At this the wife pouted, and was very cross. "'Tis too bad of you to say that. I thought you would like your wife to wear all the new fashions, and be smart like other folks."

"Nay," cried the ploughman, "my wife is much prettier than other folks, and she looks prettiest of all when she has little to adorn her. If any of these great ladies had hair like yours you may be sure they would pretty soon throw away any combs or caps or pins, so that nothing but their hair should be seen."

When her husband was gone, the wife went to her glass and looked at herself, and took out the comb and then put it in, and tried it every way. "'Tis true, for sure," said she, "my hair is very beautiful, and maybe it looks best done up as I used to wear it, still it seems a pity not to use the comb when I have bought it." So when her husband came back, she said to him, "I believe you are right, husband, and it suits me better not to have anything in my hair, but maybe if you are wanting to send a present to that cousin of yours, you would like to send her that comb. It would save buying anything fresh."

On this the ploughman laughed to himself, but he thanked his wife very much and put the comb in his pocket. In the evening after the wife had gone to bed, the ploughman took it, and put it down by the hole, and then went on smoking his pipe without waiting to see if it disappeared. But in a few minutes he heard the voice crying, "Stop! I am coming up," and saw again the gnome come through the hole and then begin to grow as before. "Now this is too bad," cried the ploughman. "What can you want now? Here I have just given you the comb you wanted, and nothing else new has come into the house." "On the contrary," answered the gnome, "I consider that you have brought a great many new things into the house since I came to live here, and I mean now to have my choice of some of them, since I do not find that you are honest enough to offer them to me. To begin with, I want your wife's hair.   I have been trying mine with that comb, and I find I can't make it do at all, and so I mean to have your wife's."

"My wife's!" gasped the ploughman.   "You must be mad!"

"Mad or not mad," replied the gnome, "I mean to have it, and, moreover, it is my due. You married without consulting me, and if I kept you to your bargain, I should have a great deal that I have not got.   Certainly your wife has the best head of hair in the house, so you must cut it off near her head and bring it all to me."

"But whatever shall I say to my wife?" cried the ploughman in distress.

"That is your look out, not mine," said the gnome.   "Anyhow you have got to give it to me.   But as the thought of it seems to annoy you I will give you a week to get it in."

The ploughman sat and thought and thought, and very sad did he feel at thinking of all his wife's beautiful hair being given away to the little gnome.

Next day he took his horse and cart, and told his wife he had to go for a long drive on business to a big town, a long way off.   It was quite the biggest town in that neighbourhood, and many very fine people lived there. At first the wife wanted to go too, but her husband said it was too far and she would be too tired, as he could not be back till very late at night.

Next morning, when they sat at breakfast, he told his wife all he had heard and seen in the big town, and then he added, " And all the very fine ladies there have now the funniest fashion."

" And what is that?" asked his wife ; " pray tell me, for I love to hear the new fashions."

" Why," said the ploughman, " 'tis with their hair. Instead of wearing it long, they have it cut quite close all round their heads, because they say it looks smarter now."

" Well, I do call that a silly fashion," said the wife ; " they can't have had much hair to consent to have had it cut off."

" No, indeed," said her husband, " and yet with some of them, they look very smart and pretty with their little curly heads."

" Much like boys, I should think," said the wife scornfully.

" No, not quite that, either," said the plough-man, " more like the pictures of angels in the old

Q

churches, and they say it is the great thing for it
to curl up all round the head, and when it does
that of itself, they are very proud of it."

" Well, then, some of them might be very proud
of mine," said the wife, " for it's as curly as may
be, and if I were to cut it short would be all in
tiny curls."

When her husband had gone to his work, the
ploughman's wife could do nothing but think of
the strange new fashion of which her husband had
told her. " I wonder how it would suit me," she
thought, and when he came in to dinner she said
to him—

" Husband, is it really true that all those fine
ladies looked very pretty and smart with their
hair short ? "

" Ay, that they did," he said ; " I was quite
surprised to see them, and I heard they said 'twas
a wonderful saving of trouble, and that their hair
could never grow untidy."

" That is true," said the wife, " yet I should be
sorry to cut mine off."

" No need that you should," said the ploughman, " and there are not many folks up here to
see if we are in the fashion or not. All the same,

" I wonder how it would look ? " and she snipped off a big bit.

you are sure to look prettier than the town ladies any way, whichever way your hair is done, for your face is prettier."

But when her husband had gone away again the wife went to her glass with the scissors in her hand. "As my husband says," she quoth, "it would be a wonderful saving of trouble, and then it would be very nice to let all the women round see that I could be in the fashion before they. I wonder how it would look?" and she snipped off abig bit. "Here goes," she cried; "after all 'tis best to follow the fashions, whatever they are," and she went on cutting till, when her husband came in, he found her with her hair all cut off beside her.

"There, husband," cried she, "do I look like the smart ladies in town?"

"Ay, that you do," he answered, "only ten times prettier; but as for all that beautiful hair, you must just give it to me, for it is so beautiful I would not let it be lost for anything," and he took up all the heap of fine gold hair and tied it together with a bright ribbon.

The wife looked at herself in the glass, and thought she really looked very nice with little

curls all round her head, and though the ploughman grieved over it in his heart, yet he was glad
he had got her hair, and thought, " Now at last
that miserable little gnome will be content, and
leave me alone." So that evening, when his wife
was gone to bed, he took the bunch of hair and
laid it near the hole, and it disappeared, and he
knew the gnome had it.

So for a time all went on quietly with the
ploughman, and he hoped he should not hear
more of the gnome, but one evening, after his
wife had gone to bed and he was in the kitchen
smoking his pipe alone, he heard the hated voice
shouting, " Stop ! I am coming up," and then he
saw the little black thing like a black beetle
coming through the hole, and all happened just
as before.

"Well, what do you want now ? " cried the
ploughman when he saw the ugly little woman in
front of him. " I have given you my wife's hair,
and surely you ought to be content."

" Not at all," said the gnome, " for I have
tried on her hair, and I find it does not suit my
complexion. I have never seen her myself, and
I don't think you any judge, but I heard you

telling her that her face was prettier than any of the town ladies. In that case you have no right to keep it for yourself. I must have your wife's face."

" My wife's face!" screamed the ploughman, " I think you must be mad. How can I give you my wife's face? And what would you do with it ? "

" Wear it," answered the gnome; "and all you have to do is to fetch your wife in here this day week, and tell her what I wish; and I will come up and scrape off as much of her face as I want."

"Why, it would kill her," cried the ploughman.

" Not at all," said the gnome, " neither would it hurt her, for she would scarcely feel my little knife; the only thing is, that when I have done, her skin will be rather black and shrivelled like my own, but as mine has been good enough for me all these years, it will surely be good enough for a common human woman. Anyhow, now you know. I must have your wife's complexion to wear with her hair, or else I go at once. And as it will be you who have broken the compact, I shall take all your wealth with me." And repeating in a deep voice, " Remember, this day week at twelve o'clock," the gnome grew small, and disappeared through the hole.

Next day the ploughman was very miserable, and whenever he looked at his wife felt inclined to burst into tears. The wife, not knowing what was amiss, tried to cheer him, and asked if he were ill. But he shook his head, and told her " no," and had not the courage to tell her the truth. Thus things went on, the ploughman growing sadder and sadder every day, till the evening before that on which the gnome had told him he must bring his wife to meet her. The ploughman was scarce able to check his sobs before his wife, and at last she came into the kitchen, and there found him crying outright.

When she saw this, she kneeled down by him, and said, " Husband, you surely do not think me a good wife, for a good wife shares all her husband's troubles. Tell me what troubles you. Two heads are better than one, and perhaps I can help you."

Then the ploughman told her all about the

hated gnome, and how he had found it in a field, and how he had promised to give it some of the best of everything, and now how it wanted her face.

At first the wife would scarcely believe it, and then she cried, " But if 'tis such a little creature why not pick it up and strangle it, or let me put my foot on it, while it is no bigger than a black beetle."

" Nay, do not think of such a thing," said her husband, "for it is ill to play tricks with fairy folk, and most likely she would kill us outright."

" But part with my face I never will," cried the wife.

" Then we will let her go and take with her the house and all our wealth, and be contented to live in my old cottage again, and be quite poor folk," said her husband.

On hearing this the wife burst into tears, and wept more bitterly than her husband, for she would not stop at all. It was in vain for him to try to cheer her and tell her that poor folk could be quite as happy as rich ones. She de-

clared she could never be happy poor. Then
when he said if she would let her face go, he
would love her just as much or more without it,
she cried that she could never be happy with a
dreadful shrivelled black skin like a monkey's.
All that night she cried, and when morning came
her skin was all red, and her eyes could scarce be
seen, so swelled were their lids, but still she cried
on all day, and her husband said nothing to
comfort her, because he did not know what to
say.   By the time it grew dark, her face was so
swelled and sore that she could not bear to touch
it, and she had cried herself almost blind, but still
the tears were rolling down.   When the time
came for the clock to strike twelve, her husband
took her hand and led her to the kitchen, and
there she sat with her face in her hands sobbing.
Just as the clock struck, they heard the voice like
thunder shouting, " Stop ! I am coming up," and
the wife peeped between her fingers and saw the
little thing no bigger than a black beetle come
through the hole and then grow, and grow, and
grow, till it was like an ugly little black woman
near a foot high. And when she saw how hideous

it was she thought, "Never, never will I consent to have a skin like that—not for millions of pounds."

The gnome did not speak to her, but said to the ploughman, "So you have brought your wife. That is a good thing, if you wish me to remain with you. So now tell her to take down her hands and let me see this face you make such a fuss about. I have my knife all ready."

And the ploughman saw that she had in her hand a tiny knife, which did not look as if it could hurt any one.

"Wife, wife," groaned the ploughman, "what shall we do?"

Then the wife looked up out of her swollen eyes, and was just going to speak, when the gnome gave a shriek. "What?" she cried, "that face! Do you mean to say that is what you think so pretty, and that I am going to change my beautiful, dry, black skin for that swollen red mass? No, indeed. You must be mad. It is a good thing that I saw it in time. I shall leave the house at once."

"Nay," cried the ploughman, "but it is you who are breaking your compact this time."

But the gnome made no reply, but scuttled down through the hole as fast as it could, and the ploughman and his wife burst out laughing for joy. And that was the last they ever saw of it, and it must have gone right away, but they knew it had left some of its luck behind it, as they both lived happily for the rest of their days.

THE END

Richard Clay & Sons, Limited, London & Bungay.

Milton Keynes UK
Ingram Content Group UK Ltd.
UKHW051920140823
426877UK00005B/197